PRAISES FOR YOU A

M000110731

"The book is an essential read for so many Christians' tiptoeing through life waiting for Heaven. Don't wait for your deathbed to learn that you are a beloved child of God. Let John take you on a journey of reflection and discovery in search of what is most important in life. Learn that you are a gift empowered by the Holy Spirit to live out your gifts in loving service, giving glory to God, your Lord, and Savior. Don't settle for just reading this book. Let it unleash the power of a life of service in His name. Why are you waiting? Don't waste another day discounting the gifts God has given you."

- **Terry Paulson**, PhD, Professional Speaker, Beloved Child of God, Author, *The Optimism Advantage*

"This book is a love story... Christ's love story to us. John Bentley shows us Christ's love in Scripture, stories, and messages of love. Through a personal tragedy, Jesus woke John up and sent him out to teach each how loved and gifted how we are. Don't miss John's energizing message, passionate plea, and solid teachings. This is a gem to be treasured. You will be inspired to identify your gifts and serve more deeply through them."

- **Elizabeth Jeffries**, CSP. CPAE Speaker Hall of Fame, Author, *What Exceptional Executives Need to Know*

"What an amazing discovery is awaiting you as you open these pages of transformational realities! John Bentley created this 'Box of Truths' that are just for YOU. He has verified every truth with a solid Biblical proof text. In addition, you will find fascinating stories that underscore these Truths for your everyday life. And imagine this: YOU are walking in the will of God for your life at this very moment, but you just might not know that! (Proverbs 16:9) Chapter by chapter, you will discover that YOU are truly a GIFT of God to this needy world!! A life of miraculous discoveries lies ahead of you as your eyes are opened to the GIFT you really are!!!"

> - **Glenna Salsbury**, CSP, CPAE, Cavett Recipient, Author, *The Art the Fresh Start*, Past President of the National Speakers Association

"John Bentley's book, *You Are A GIFT*, spoke directly to my heart. I believe it has a message for every single person on this planet. It answers fundamental human questions such as 'Why am I here?' 'Who am I?', and 'What am I called to be and do?' Founded upon biblical truths, John writes with simplicity and clarity and presents a gift to the reader ... a gift that affirms the value of his or her life and the value we are called by our Creator to give to others in each person's own unique way. This book will be of great use for all those who are seeking to find themselves as well as all those who seek to enrich and bless the lives of others – teenagers, parents, teachers, counselors, and pastors among others. John Bentley is living his message. Thank you, John, for using your talents to give a gift to me and to the world."

> - **Dilip R. Abayasekara**, Ph.D., M.Div., DTM, Accredited Speaker, Past International President, Toastmasters International, Pastor

"If you are looking for clear, specific, and encouraging answers to what it means to be strong in your faith and to walk daily with God, then you need to read *You Are A GIFT*. If you are looking for guidance on how to use the gifts God has given you in service to his children, then you need to read *You Are A GIFT*. John Bentley has provided us with an uplifting and challenging plan for us to glorify God through the gifts HE has given each of us. A must read for everyone who truly wants to be the person God made you to be."

   - Al Walker, Certified Speaking Professional, Author, and Member of the Speakers Hall of Fame

"If you only read one book this year, make it this one! John Bentley's *You Are A GIFT* is a powerful book which reminds us of all the importance of continuing to seek and understand God's Kingdom and the marvel of His gifts, one of which is YOU."

   - Don Hutson, Speaker, #1 Best-Selling Co-Author, *The One Minute Entrepreneur*

"Give yourself a GIFT. And get this book. See how John uses the full range of emotions to help you feel better about yourself and what you want to become. John is a word smith that will inspire you to reach new heights helping others with your GIFT. This book is truly a tremendous, uplifting spiritual read."

   - Patrick O'Dooley, Certified Speaking Professional

"This book is a 'Five Star' rating! Every student of the Bible should own and read; *You Are A GIFT*. I devoured and assimilated every word of it! I highly recommend this book to you. I believe that everyone will find out what a PRECIOUS JOY it is to discover their GIFT and how YOU too can be that special GIFT for someone else!"

   - Fernand Saint-Louis, Pastor, Evangelist, French Translator for Billy Graham Crusades

"*You Are A GIFT* is a complete demonstration of John Bentley not only listening to his hurting heart to help others from the loss of his daughter Natalie but also following God's plan to serve. *You Are a GIFT* is more than a good read and should be used as a teaching tool for us during unimaginable struggles."

   - James Perdue, Ed.D, Professor of Perseverance, Podcast Host and Speaker

"From the opening words, *You Are a GIFT* takes us on a gut-wrenching, yet simultaneously uplifting journey, that dives head-first into the real issues of life. This book is an amazing tribute to John Bentley's late daughter, Natalie, and her God-breathed gift for loving and encouraging others. But its more than that. *You Are a GIFT* is a real-life story about John's personal journey through sorrow and loss to face his own life failures and shortcomings. Page after page we are reminded that we are called to be gifts to those around us…but must develop our own spiritual gifts to do so. With scriptural references on literally every page, great effort is taken to help readers understand God's individual calling on our lives, the role of spiritual warfare in the life of the believer, as well as the unique gifts that God has given each of us. Most importantly, we are beautifully pointed to the Author of the Gift, Jesus Christ, and reminded that He desires for us to become everything he intended us to be…and then to share it with everyone! Birthed from a heart-gripping experience of love and loss, *You Are a GIFT* is a hands-on tool for discovering your spiritual gifts. John uses his personal journey to remind us that God works in our darkest hours to forge us into His image, and then calls us to pour ourselves into others to make an eternal difference. *You Are a GIFT* helps us do just that and will forever change the way you view God's calling on your life."

   - L. Lavon Gray, PhD, MBA, CSP

"So many of us go through life searching for answers to questions like :"Who am I?" "Why am I here?" and "what is my purpose?" Some get discouraged because the answers don't come soon enough, loud enough, or clear enough. We pray to God, and "crickets." May I humbly suggest that some of us need to search no more. John Bentley's book, *You Are A GIFT* brings insight to all these questions. He would be the first to tell you that he is merely sharing the wisdom of God that came to him from the most painful of experiences, the loss of his child. In this raw and well-written book, you will read, hear, and feel the words of God. You will find deep insight and answers to these tough questions above. You will discover and learn how to use the GIFTs God has bestowed upon YOU."

   - Kevin R. McNulty, MA - Speaker, Coach, and Author, *The Gap Between Two Worlds…*

"Seems like, other than John 3:16, the verse most often quoted by believers comes from Romans, verse 8:28. And the first part of that verse seems to be most talked about: knowing all things work together for good, if we love God! And I believe that!! But I also firmly believe we are called for His Purpose while we are still here. "Love God and respond to His calling for His Purpose." And John Bentley's latest book is inspired by that calling. John crafts Scripture and application into such strong encouragement for each of us to realize our uniqueness in Christ, the talents, and abilities He has uniquely given to us, and the purpose He has for us. *You Are A GIFT* is truly an inspired gift, helping us to better understand God's specific calling and purpose for our lives and how He prepares us to express His love in serving others."

- Jim Flinn, Co-Director, Church On The Lake – Guntersville

"John turned the tragic loss of his daughter into a powerful message of spiritual healing and redemption through GOD and JESUS CHRIST that all can now experience through this work!"

- Apostle Kelvin Franklin, New Testament Church Movement
Ministry and Author, *Paul, The Moses of the New Testament*

"Living is a process in which God is always worthy of your praise, of which faith never concedes. God's will by faith cornerstones the believer's lifestyle in responsibility to Himself that true meaning and purpose is found in the direst of life's experiences. The Holy Spirit specializes in producing well even from unfortunate incidents. The reactionary lifestyle lives from event to event, allowing circumstances to dictate its gratitude, faith, hope, and praise. Through the writing of this masterpiece, *You Are A Gift,* my spiritual son, Minister John Bentley, brilliantly benefits the understanding that even the worst of occurrences in the long run and light of eternity can be best at advantaging the highest good."

"Occasionally the blessings of your calling may come through suffering in ways you don't understand or decipher? Many times it's what crushes your heart that may be perfectly utilized to generate the highest good, which in the case of what's most unwanted, you can realize you are a gift."

- **Apostle Darryl Jackson**, Church of the Firstborn Ministries, Inc.

"What a wealth of wisdom in one place! This is like a play book for living a fulfilling life! John begins with the question: Have you ever stopped to think and examine how precious your life is?

"In the middle lies the wisdom that makes the difference between surviving in this world versus living a fulfilling life by using your gifts to serve…wait for it…others!"

"What else will you learn? About your Creator, your enemy, and your defense against spiritual battle. About the purpose of gifts and what gifts are yours. Then there is the gem I wish I had learned earlier in my own life about empowerment – John writes:

Until we finally come to the point in our lives where we finally recognize and say, "God that's it, I can't do this anymore, I don't have the strength and ability to run my own life." That ironically, is the beginning whereby God can continue His work in you!"

"Take advantage of John's wisdom and encouragement to reflect and ponder. Begin living a fulfilling life today!"

- **Susan Elder**, Site Coordinator, Christian Women's Job Corp of Madison AL, Inc.

YOU ARE A GIFT!

made in God's Image to

Fulfill your Talent in

service to others.

By John Bentley

Forward By Naomi Rhode, CSP, CPAE
Speaker Hall of Fame

Publisher: You Are A GIFT Foundation

Request for information should be addressed to:

John Bentley, 1005 Ashworth St NE, Hartselle, AL 35640 or email: john@youareagift.foundation

ISBN: 978-1-7320328-2-8

Bible Scripture Advisor: Phil R. Taylor

Edited by: Pastor Beverly Jackson

Interior design by: James Perdue, Ed. D.

Dedicated to my daughter Natalie Lively (Tigee)

Even in your darkest hour you used your God-given gifts to serve others in their time of need.

Contents

Acknowledgements

Thanks to people who use their God-given gifts to serve others by living and loving like Jesus. You make the world is a better place! What made *You Are A GIFT* possible is the people who came alongside me during my transformation journey.

First and foremost, glory and praise to our Heavenly Father who planted the word *GIFT* in my heart after He used the death of my adult daughter, Natalie Lively, to awaken me to my true identity in Christ.

Thank you to my daughter and son-in-law, Krista and Kendall Prestidge. You chose to become instant parents to Alex when his mom and your sister, Natalie, passed away. As a result, you welcomed five-year-old Alex into your home in January 2011. He has grown into a healthy and happy young man because of your unconditional love.

To my wife Laura, I am eternally grateful God brought us together. You knew how to love me through my grief while encouraging me to write You Are A GIFT. In addition, you served as a sounding board during the writing and publishing process, for which I am forever thankful.

Without the experiences and support of my peers and friends, this book would not exist. You've allowed me to share how God uses adversity in our lives to transform us more into the likeness of Christ Jesus so we can share the good news of the Gospel to a broken and fallen world. Thank you to Phil R. Taylor, Kevin McNulty, RJ Jackson, James Perdue, Maxine Wilson, Jim Flynn, Susan Elder, Charles Webber, Roger Alves, Bob Brumm, Dave Gorden, Harold Spradlin, Apostle Darryl Jackson, Pastor Beverly Jackson, Apostle Kelvin Franklin and Dr. Frank Marshall.

Foreword

Dear Reader......

Do you know that YOU are a 'GIFT'.....?

Do you know that YOU are GOD's unique, one of a kind 'GIFT' .....to His world through Him to YOUR world?

Do you know that He chose you, before the foundations of the earth?

Do you really dwell in His Son's atonement for you?

Have you ever been startled by the mundaneness of trying to meet the world's expectations,

be loved by 'them', instead of living in His expectations and being totally loved by Him?

This book is just that....a startling realization of the magnificence of dwelling in

God's amazing love, goodness, grace, and blessing.

Knowing His Word, and living His Word, His Life, His Power are two different things.

Have you ever truly awakened to that reality?

John Bentley did!

A powerful awakening that changed his life, and gave him the Holy Spirit's prodding, passion, and purpose to share this journey of 'awakening' with you, and with me.

This is not 'just a treatise' on Theology, huge as that indeed is.

This is a dramatic shift in Living 'the 'GIFT'...

3

His Gift of endowing us with everything we need to minister His love to a hurting world.

John is a believer, yes,

John is a disciple, yes,

But…John has been transformed to live the remainder of his life walking in God's precious indwelling love and leading.

I pray that you will sense a new awakening, perhaps even a transformation, also, as you soak in the reality of God's love for You!

He has 'gifted you'…so that undeniably YOU are a 'GIFT'!

Indeed, this is not an ordinary 'book'…this is a book about the 'BOOK', the Person of Jesus Christ, the indwelling of His Spirit, and God's amazing love for you!

Amen and amen,

Naomi Rhode, CSP, CPAE Speaker Hall of Fame

(Mostly loved by God, a forgiven saint, living for Him through His power and peace.)

Introduction

On my 50th birthday, I sensed God was going to do something significant in my life. I saw myself speaking to thousands of people. The next thought that ran through my mind was, Lord it's about time You give me the recognition and rewards I deserve!

On December 11th, 2010, just 28 days later, I received confirmation of the something significant - a phone call from my daughter Krista. I answered and said, "Hello, Sweetheart, how are you?" I expected her to wish Laura and me a happy anniversary. Instead, I heard, "Dad, Natalie's dead!"

Natalie is my oldest daughter and the mother of my first grandson, Alex. Only 15 days from her 29th birthday, she lost her battle with the complications caused by prescription drug addiction.

During her funeral, the opening words of the Pastor were from Philippians 4:4, *"Rejoice in the Lord always; again, I say, Rejoice!"* Upon hearing those words, I felt a burst of anger. My thoughts began to race. Who are you to tell me to rejoice in the Lord always? Why would I rejoice over the death of my daughter? How dare you! I later came to accept and appreciate, *"And we know that God causes all things work together for good to those who love God, to those who are called according to his purpose"* (Romans 8:28).

A few days passed, and I gained the courage to view Natalie's Facebook page. I quickly discovered how I missed one crucial detail about my precious daughter. She had a special gift that made other people feel truly loved, valued, and deeply appreciated. I was astonished to see just how many lives she had touched. As I continued to scroll, I saw one posting after another, well over 60 people whose young lives Natalie positively impacted.

For the next couple of months, there was one thought that God kept on my heart. Life is precious, and with each life comes the expression of being a gift and a blessing to others. Natalie's God-given talents included the gift of helping and the gift of service. Despite her declining health condition, she served others by

- cleaning their homes,
- cooking meals for them,
- watching their children while they worked, and
- listening to others' burdens and reminding them they are a precious child of God.

The word **GIFT** became stronger and stronger through this realization and now is an acronym for **G**od's **I**mage **F**ulfill **T**alent.

I am proud of Natalie and how she served others with her God-given **GIFT**s. Unfortunately, it took her death for me to realize that I did not know my daughter beyond being a physical presence in her life. You see, during her illness, I was there to provide financial support, ensure she and Alex had food on the table, and visit her from time to time each year. I did so to feel good about myself and ignored her addiction. I chose not to be

6

present emotionally and failed to be there for Natalie during the darkest moments of her life.

The Awakening

Most assuredly, God revealed through Natalie's death that I had an identity crisis. I was living for the world and got my self-worth from possessions, positions, and people. As long as I owned the best car, the biggest house, the fanciest clothes, had the most important job, college degrees, and the right people liked me, I felt worthy. As you may imagine, I had low self-esteem and looked for external validation to feel okay about myself.

I now rejoice and praise God for using Natalie's death as a spark to awaken me. God showed me a gap existed between me knowing the truths about who He says I am and living His truths. What I believed about myself was affected by my life experiences and the way the world defines success.

My beliefs from a childhood of *I can do nothing right, I must be perfect, and children are to be seen and not heard* followed me into adulthood. To be fair, my mother and father never said they did not love me. They wanted me always to give my best, which translated into, *I am not good enough.* Believing I could not satisfy my earthly parents, especially my father, created a belief there is no way God will love me.

According to Ephesians 1, we have been blessed with every spiritual blessing; we have been chosen, adopted, redeemed, forgiven, grace-lavished and unconditionally loved and accepted. We are pure, blameless, and forgiven. We have received the hope of spending eternity with God. When we are in Christ, we can never alter these aspects of our identity by what we do.

By believing the promises of Ephesians 1, I came to realize, that I had surrendered enough to accept Jesus as my savior but not my Lord and remained comfortable living for the world. Now, I know God called me to **COMPLETELY** surrender and make Jesus the Lord and Savior of my life so He can transform me more into the likeness of Christ to share the good news of the Gospel and further His Kingdom. Praise God that I am no longer under the law and think *I must be perfect* for God to love me. My purpose now is to use my God-given **GIFT**s to serve others and glorify the Lord.

Why This Book

When you live out your identity based on how God sees you, the need to find your self-worth from external sources is no longer necessary. You now live a life of peace and joy and do not change who you are based on others' opinions, professional success, how you feel, and all the other ways you define significance. Because you now experience God's unconditional love, you fearlessly share His love with others.

On December 11th, 2020, I had a dream. I was standing beside people on their death bed about to take their last breath. While professing to be a Christian, they were frightened, not knowing if they would be in Heaven upon their death. The fear in their eyes broke my heart as I realized this would have been me until God intervened through my daughter's death. I do not want **ANYONE** to feel this way on their death bed.

I want them to look back and see how they glorified God by using their **GIFT**s to serve others instead of for personal gain. Then and only then will they be at peace and filled with joy, knowing they will be in Heaven kneeling before God, hearing "Well done my good and faithful servant!" as they draw their last breath.

Your Brother in Christ,

John

P.S. I pray you will meditate on the Biblical truths you read throughout this book, fully surrender to the promptings of the Holy Spirit, and allow God to transform you more into the likeness of Christ every day. May His grace, love, mercy, and peace give you the courage to boldly serve others with your God-given **GIFT**s for His glory. In Jesus' name, AMEN.

Chapter 1

You are a GIFT

"Thanks be to God for His indescribable gift!"
(2 Corinthians 9:15)

Have you ever stopped to think, and examine how precious your life is? God's Word declares in Ephesians 2:10 that you are *His workmanship*! Scripture shares that you've been created anew in Christ Jesus, which He had planned long before you were conceived and before the earth's foundation was formed. That is how well thought-out and constructed your life is.

In addition to that, have you ever stopped to consider, just how unique your life is, as well? You are also one of a kind, no one from the beginning from creation to this day has been or is exactly like you. No one has the exact combined set of unique experiences, background, DNA makeup and gifts you have.

Like a snowflake, you are indeed one of a kind. Trillions of snowflakes have beautifully fallen from the sky; yet, fascinatingly enough, scientists to this day have never been able to discover even one that is precisely the same. Isn't that something?

It is as if God, the Creator, used snowflakes as a metaphor for our lives. Just as there are billions of unique snowflakes, you too are one of a kind.

In fact, not only are you one of a kind in the midst of all the billions of people who lived and died throughout history, but you are nothing short of a miracle!

Scientists have calculated that the odds of you being born is at the very least 1 in 400 trillion. If that doesn't awaken your perspective into the preciousness of life, I don't know what does.

How many of us take this incredible gift of life for granted?

How many of us just go about our way in life without really giving thought to the incredible privilege it is to be alive?

Furthermore, in Genesis 1:27 we read, *"So God created man in his own image, in the image of God He created him; male and female He created them."*

How wonderful to know God loves us so much that He made us in His image.

David in Psalms expands on this great marvel when he states God's magnificent intimacy and care for your life, saying,

"For You created my innermost parts;
You wove me in my mother's womb.
I will give thanks to You, because I am awesomely and
wonderfully made;
Wonderful are Your works,
And my soul knows it very well.
My frame was not hidden from You
When I was made in secret,
And skillfully formed in the depths of the earth;
Your eyes have seen my formless substance;

And in Your book were written

All the days that were ordained for me,

When as yet there was not one of them.

How precious also are Your thoughts for me, God!

How vast is the sum of them!

Were I to count them, they would outnumber the sand.

When I awake, I am still with You"

(Psalm 139:13-18).

Listen, God knows you intimately. He even knows you more than you know yourself. God has been with you from the very beginning, as far back as when you were in your mother's womb. He designed you to reflect His own image. He loves you and has an incredible plan for your life.

The Bible states that God knew you and was present as He formed you in your mother's womb. In Ephesians 1:4, we discover that He also knew you and had a magnificent design for your life even before the foundations of the earth were created. *"...just as he chose us in Him before the foundation of the world, that we would be holy and blameless before Him. In love."*

Yes, we were made in God's image, designed even before He made the world, so that we may glorify Him and live a full and meaningful life by serving others. Do you realize just how special, unique, and super-blessed you are? That God knew you and had you in mind, even before He created the universe.

The ultimate gift is that you are created in His image, which he predestined long before even the world was created, so that you

13

would have a relationship with Him as dear children and as children made in His image would reflect His very character and nature in all that you are and all that you do.

It is for this reason that in 2 Corinthians 5:20, we are called *His ambassadors.* We have, in essence, become the head, the heart and the hands of God to declare His wonders and His great love.

Jesus, who is God, made flesh, who lived, died, and was raised from the dead and reconciled Himself to us describes our relationship with Him in these terms, *"I am the vine, you are the branches ..."* (John 15:5), thus meaning that we are inherently connected to Him as an extension and reflection of His character and good works.

Many of us have heard the endearing term "He is a chip off the old block" when someone refers to a child in relation to his or her parents, as to say, he is just like his father or mother in character and behavior.

In the same way, we're created in the image of God, having His behavior and character designed and destined unto good works.

It is for this reason that Jesus implores us in Matthew 5:48, that we are to, "... *be perfect, as your heavenly Father is perfect."* The original ancient Greek term of the word "perfect" is translated to mean "complete."

In essence, Jesus is pleading with us to live up to our calling as children of the living God. We are called to mirror God in His character and moral excellence. That is what it means to be created in the image of God, it is a calling to be the reflection of God in this world.

Though we are complete in Him, it does not mean that in fact, we will be perfect, since our nature is still marred by sin. Thankfully, we are being made perfect through the process of sanctification, which means to be shaped and molded in His perfect and complete image, which will come into full manifestation when we see Him face-to-face.

While we await that glorious day, God provide us with a helper, the Holy Spirit to live our calling, just as Jesus did, to ultimately become perfect, just as He is perfect

John Newton, author of the wonderful hymn, 'Amazing Grace' reflected this reality and sanctifying process when he stated this, "I am not what I ought to be, I am not what I want to be, I am not what I hope to be in another world, but still I am not what I once used to be, and by the grace of God I am what I am."[1]

What John Newton stated was the experience and the process that, though he had admittedly not yet arrived, he was being increasingly shaped and molded into the perfect image of God. And the process will be finalized and complete when we meet Him in heaven.

The Apostle Paul in Philippians 3:12-14 reflects the same truth when he states, *"Not that I have already grasped it all or have already become perfect, but I press if I may also take hold of that for which I was even taken hold of by Christ Jesus. Brothers and sisters, I do not regard myself as having taken hold of it yet; but one thing I do: forgetting what lies behind, and reaching forward to what lies ahead, I press on toward the goal for the prize of the upward calling of God in Christ Jesus."*

Salvation according to the Bible is three-fold in the sense that we have been described as beloved children of God, who have been, are being saved, and will be saved. Ultimately, our call and our gift in this world is to reflect the character of God. That is what it means to be created in His image.

There are three facets to our life exemplified as a gift, and they are:

1. We are a gift **from** God.
2. We are a gift **to** God.
3. We are a gift to **others.**

Firstly, our life is a gift from God. Romans 6:23, states, *"For the wages of sin is death, but the gracious gift of God is eternal life in Christ Jesus our Lord".* Because of God's grace and mercy received from Him, we have eternal life.

For years I asked, "What must I *do* to earn the right to enter into the Kingdom of God?" Because of my thinking, I had a legalistic view of God and was searching the bible for a checklist of here's what you *'Do'* and *'Don't Do'* to be welcomed into heaven. As you may imagine, I was miserable. Why, because I did not understand you don't earn everlasting life. My life changed the moment I acknowledged, that all joy and the fullness of life come from God.

16

Please do not underestimate what God has given you. The world itself, and all the blessings that are on our earth, God gave to you. You never made it or earned it, and your individual life is a gift. Our abilities and everything we have is a gift from God and the greatest gift is eternal salvation through faith in Jesus Christ.

Secondly, we are a gift to God. The essence of this statement is reflected so well in Romans 12:1 whereby we read, *"Therefore I urge you, brothers and sister by the mercies of God, to present your bodies a living and holy sacrifice, acceptable to God, which is your spiritual service of worship."*

How could we not out of this profound sense of awareness, love, and appreciation, give it all back to Him? It has been said, "Our life is a gift from God, and what we do with it is our gift to God."

I believe there is no other scene in Scripture that accurately depicts the intensity of the worthiness of God, and rightful response to Him for the life, grace, mercy, and goodness He has bestowed upon us. The scene is found in Revelation 4:10-11. *"...the twenty-four elders will fall down before Him who sits on the throne, and will worship Him who lives forever and ever, and will cast their crowns before the throne, saying, "Worthy are You, our Lord and our God, to receive glory, and honor, and power; for You created all things, and because of Your will they existed, and were created."*

It is the intensity of that moment, when we are confronted with the awesomeness of God's power, grace, and glory that we will

17

fully see the truth in Him. Although He has promised those who love Him with a reward and a crown of glory, our hearts will be overcome with humility, whereby the only impulse that is warranted would be to cast our crowns before Him with a sense of unmeasurable gratitude, in recognition of His love, power, mercy, and grace, and cry out *"Worthy are You, our Lord and our God, to receive glory, honor, and power; You created all things, and because of Your will they existed, and were created"* (Revelation 4:11).

The sooner we realize and experience this great truth, that it is God who deserves all the praise and glory, the sooner our lives will be activated according to His will.

What can you give to someone who has given you everything, every good and perfect gift? The answer is provided when Jesus was confronted by the Pharisees with the question, what is the greatest commandment? Jesus replied, *"and you shall love the Lord your God with all your heart, and with all your soul, and with all your mind, and with all your strength"* (Mark 12:30).

The Spurgeon Study Bible shares, *'With all your heart'* means intensely. *'With all your soul'* means sincerely, most lovingly, and *'With all your strength'* means with all our energy, with every faculty, with every possibility of our nature.[2]

Yes, when we recognize the enormous, unspeakable grace, and the love and generosity of God, how could we not intensely love Him with all our heart? How are we to sincerely love from our soul, put forth all our energy and fully use our mind to gain God's understanding and blessings? To give our gift to God requires us to seek the Kingdom of God above all else.

- *Think and learn about the Kingdom of God.*
- *Seek God and you will find His Kingdom.*
- *Seek the Kingdom of God and you will love God more and more.*
- *Seek the Kingdom of God and your perspectives will change for the better.*
- *Seek the Kingdom of God daily and you will receive what you need.*

Remember this is made possible, because God first loved us and sent His only begotten Son to die for our sins. However, Jesus did not stop here.

There is a third facet of our life depicted as a gift to others, and it is found in Jesus's next statement to the Pharisees, *"the second is like it, 'You shall love your neighbor as yourself'"* (Matthew 22:39).

We are to offer our lives in love to one another. We are instructed not only to love one another, but to love one another as Christ loved us, as God has loved us. And with that not only are we to love one another, but we are to:

- *Encourage one another*
- *Pray for one another*
- *Teach one another*
- *Honor one another*

19

These are just of a few of the 59 times in the New Testament we are to treat one another in this way, and in terms of sharing your life and your gift, we are exhorted in 1 Peter 4:10 that, *"As each one has received a special gift, employ it in serving one another as good stewards of the multifaceted grace of God."*

Isn't that beautiful?!

The interesting part about this commandment is that it is completely counter to what we see in the world. People in the world are constantly looking out for themselves, the great *'I or Me'* mentality. The great *'I or Me'* defines my early adult life. I wanted the best car, the biggest house, the most important job, and for people to look up to me. Because I was only looking out for myself and what I could get from others, I constantly struggled, was frustrated, and had very few opportunities for success. Peace and joy were not possible because I continuously strived to prove I was better than others. And this stemmed from a poor self-worth, and always believing I was not good enough no matter what I accomplished. My identity was in the world and what I could get instead of applying my gifts to serve others and glorify God. Summed up, I had an identity crisis.

The world is also self-absorbed, self-centered; and yet, a self-seeking society is exactly what the Bible prophesies. In 2 Timothy 3:1-4, we read that, *"... People will be lovers of self, lover of money, boastful, arrogant, ...,"* when really the secret to joy and to life is not achieved in what we do for ourselves but what we do and can give to others.

There is an ancient parable referred to as *'The Allegory Long Spoons'* that exemplifies the powerful principle that comes with serving one another. One day a man said to God, "God, I would like to know what Heaven and Hell are like." God showed the man two doors. Inside the first one, in the middle of the room, was a large round table with a large pot of vegetable stew. It smelled delicious and made the man's mouth water, but the people sitting at the table were thin and sickly. They appeared to be famished. They were holding spoons with very long handles, and each found it possible to reach into the pot and stew and take a spoonful, but because the handle was longer than their arms, they could not get the spoons back into their mouths.

The man shuddered at the sight of their misery and suffering. God said, "You have seen Hell."

Behind the second door, the room appeared exactly the same. There was the large round table with the large pot of vegetable stew that made the man's mouth water. The people have the same long-handled spoons, but they were well nourished and plump, laughing and talking.

The man said, "I don't understand." God smiled, "It's simple", he said. "Love only requires one skill. These people learned early on to share and feed one another. While the greedy only think of themselves." [3]

Although this parable is only fictional, and not to be taken as a biblical truth, the principle of this illustration does ring true. Scripture is filled with insights that point to the power of serving

21

each other. In Proverbs 11:25 (NIV), we read, *"A generous person will prosper; whoever refreshes others will be refreshed."* The people behind the second door were joyful and well-nourished because they were not focused on themselves but rather on the wellbeing of one another. They gave of themselves to one another, and everyone was filled.

In 1 Corinthians 2:14 (NIV), we read, *"The person without the Spirit does not accept the things that come from the Spirit of God but considers them foolishness and cannot understand them because they are discerned only through the Spirit."*

The principle that our life is designed in such a way, by our Creator, that we are here and at our best, and our highest level of joy and function, when we are caught up in giving our lives away as a gift of service to others. The truth of God's wisdom is that we discover through the guidance of the Holy Spirit that, in fact, it is more blessed to give than to receive.

My grandmother, Eunice, known as Granny, was a wonderful example of someone who always gave of herself and her resources. She was the mother of nine children and grandmother to 21 grandchildren. Two of her children died during birth, one was killed during WWII and three grandchildren died as well. She had no formal education yet possessed much wisdom. To make ends meet and provide for everyone, she grew a garden and bartered the vegetables with others for milk, eggs, beef, and pork.

Despite living on a fixed income and experiencing numerous tragedies, she put the needs of others before her own. Every

Sunday, 15-20 of us would gather at her house. She prepared a feast for us using her limited resources and never complained. Granny took the time to sit and talk with each of us. She loved us all in ways that made us feel important. In the community, Granny would provide clothing and help those less fortunate than herself.

Through and through, Granny was living the message of Philippians 2:3-5 that states, *"do nothing through selfish or empty conceit, but with humility, consider one another as more important than yourselves; do not merely look out for your own personal interests, but also the interests of others. Have this attitude in yourselves which was also in Christ Jesus."*

As Granny continued to console us and tenderly guide us with godly wisdom, I could remember that, whenever I became upset because something wasn't going my way she would say, "John, life is nothing but a series of problem-solving activities. How you respond determines the outcome you get. Now, be happy you have a problem to solve." Looking back, I remember Granny always being at peace and full of joy no matter the circumstances.

Now, as stated in 1 Corinthians 1:22-24, the person without the Spirit cannot even begin to understand the principle of humility and putting others before yourself; it is completely foreign to their own nature and considered foolish.

Ah, but you, a child of God, have been called out of darkness into His marvelous light. Because of Him, we no longer think or behave as the world does, for we have been given the gift of life. We are a new creation, in Christ Jesus, and for this reason, we are exhorted in Romans 12:2, *"And do not be conformed to this world, but be transformed by the renewing of your mind, so that you may prove what the will of God is, that which is good and acceptable and perfect."*

As redeemed children of God, we are called to and live on a whole different dimension than that of the world.

- *What God calls wise, the world calls foolish,*
- *What God regards as a strength, the world regards it as weakness,*
- *What God calls rich and blessed, the world calls poor.*

It is all topsy-turvy where the world is concerned, but God says, in Isaiah 55:8-9,

"For my thoughts are not your thoughts,

Nor are your ways My ways," declares the Lord.

"For as the heavens are higher than the earth,

So are My ways higher than your ways

And my thoughts than your thoughts."

Listen, as a child of the living God, you have been endowed with wisdom, power, and gifts that are beyond measure and comprehension. You are as 1 Peter 2:9 declares, *"...a chosen people, a royal priesthood, a holy nation, a people for God's own possession, so that you may proclaim the excellencies of Him who has called you out of darkness into His marvelous light."*

Because you are in Christ, you are a new creature, super-charged with God's presence to transform lives through His power, wherever you go and whomever you meet   You are God's ambassador, a channel of His love and gift to the world.

Saint Francis of Assisi put it in the form of this prayer that sums up our calling as living sacrifices to God and thus, to others.

"Lord, make me an instrument of your peace:

where there is hatred, let me sow love;

where there is injury, pardon;

where there is doubt, faith;

where there is despair, hope;

where there is darkness, light;

where there is sadness, joy.

O divine Master, grant that I may not so much seek

to be consoled as to console,

to be understood as to understand,

to be loved as to love.

For it is in giving that we receive." [4]

To give, that is what we have been called to do, to give your life away, as a gift to God and to others. That is why the word "gift" can be summed up in this way, that You are a **GIFT**, made in **G**od's **I**mage to **F**ulfill your **T**alent in service to others.

REFLECTION

Review (What struck you personally?)

Revelation (What is God saying to you?)

Response (What are you going to do today)

Chapter 2

Author of the GIFT

"Every good thing given, and every perfect gift is from above, coming down from the Father of lights, with whom can be no variation, or shifting shadow."

(James 1:17)

To fully understand and appreciate what it means to be made in God's image, we need to know who the source of that image is, don't we?

Who is God? What is He like? What are His characteristics? Only once we have begun to uncover who God is can we start to understand the rich and profound depths of what it means to be a reflection of Him.

Yet, before we enter this glorious discovery of God's attributes, I believe that the most wonderful, intimate AND comforting aspect of God is that He is our Father. Imagine the God of our universe, who put the sun, the moon, the sky, the stars, the planets, along with earth and all of its inhabitants into motion, did so out of intimate love.

A beautiful melody written by John W. Peterson entitled, 'He Owns the Cattle (On A Thousand Hills)'[1], epitomizes this beautiful truth in such an endearing way. It goes like this,

27

"He owns the cattle on a thousand hills,

The wealth in every mine;

He owns the rivers and the rocks and rills,

The sun and stars that shine.

Wonderful riches, more than tongue can tell;

He is my Father so they're mine as well;

He owns the cattle on a thousand hills;

I know that He will care for me."

And it is true! Psalm 50:10-11 says, *"For every animal of the forest is Mine, The cattle on a thousand hills. I know every bird in the mountains, And everything that moves in field is Mine."*

God knows you. He knows you to the extent that *"... the hairs of your head are all counted"* (Matthew 10:30).

Romans 8:14-15 states, *"For all who are being led by the Spirit of God, these are sons and daughters of God. For you have not received the spirit a spirit of slavery, leading to fear again, but you have received a spirit of adoption, as sons and daughters by which we cry out, "Abba! Father!"*

Oh how beautiful, that we should be called, as a result of His amazing grace and adoption, the children of God! God is not only the creator of this universe, but more intimately, He is our loving Father, whereby we call Him "Abba."

Abba is a beautiful and wonderfully intimate term. This Aramaic word means "Father," yet it implies a deeper meaning expressing profound affection, confidence, and trust, as a relationship of a loving father to his child. Its relation to childlike

28

faith can be translated to the term "Papa," referring to a tender and trusting relationship a small child has with their father.

Interestingly enough, it is also the very same term that Jesus uses to address God while he suffered and prayed in the Garden of Gethsemane. Before His capture, He cried out *"Abba, Father,"* as indicated in Mark 14:36.

The God we have a relationship with is not a God that is distant, a speculation of our minds, but rather, He is close to us. In Matthew 7:9-11, we read, *"Or what person is there among you who, when his son asks him for a loaf of bread, will give him a stone? Or if he asks for a fish, he will not give him a snake, will he? So if you despite, being evil, know how to give good gifts to your children, how much more will your Father who is in heaven give good things to those who ask Him!"*

To those of us who have or had loving fathers, just take the experience you have been blessed with, and multiply it by a million. That is how much your Heavenly Father loves you and cares for you!

For those of us, perhaps a little like myself, who struggled in the formative days of our lives to know and experience that kind of love from a father, know this, that your earthly father most likely is or was a wounded man, and incapable of reflecting the sort of love you deserved. It is not his fault; he just was not able, for whatever reason, to give you something which he himself did not have.

Yet for those of us who may feel that way, there is comforting news. For scripture itself clearly states that God has a special place in His heart for those who feel this way or have found themselves fatherless. Psalm 68:5 states that God is, *"A father of the fatherless."* and what better hands to be in than in the care of God our Father?

This concept is emphasized in the way in which Jesus teaches us how we ought to pray as read in Matthew 6:9-13. He begins with the personal, and endearing title of *"Our Father."* He continues with:

"Pray, then, in this way:

"Our Father who is in heaven,

Hallowed be Your name.

Your kingdom come.

Your will be done,

On earth as it is in heaven.

Give us this day, our daily bread.

And forgive us our debts, as we also have forgiven our debtors.

And do not lead us not into temptation but deliver us from the evil one.

For Yours is the Kingdom, and the power and the glory forever. Amen."

Another place we find the nature of God's heart displayed is in the parable of the Prodigal Son. Listen to what and how the father responded when the lost son began his journey home. In Luke 15:20, he, *"felt compassion for him, and ran and embraced him and kissed him."*

What a scene! To think that after everything his son demanded and every action he took, that his father would still show him love, grace and mercy. When the son had squandered his savings and disparaged his family, his father still welcomed him back home. This act of forgiveness and show of solidarity with his disobedient son remains to this day as the ultimate model of what Christ's love for us is like.

The power of this parable is so beautiful, and profoundly touching that it must be retold in its entirety. Here it is as recorded in Luke 15:11-31 (NIV)

"Jesus continued: "There was a man who had two sons. The younger one said to his father, 'Father, give me my share of the estate.' So, he divided his property between them."

"Not long after that, the younger son got together all he had, set off for a distant country and there squandered his wealth in wild living. After he had spent everything, there was a severe famine in that whole country, and he began to be in need. So, he went and hired himself out to a citizen of that country, who sent him to his fields to feed pigs. He longed to fill his stomach with the pods that the pigs were eating, but no one gave him anything."

"I will set out and go back to my father and say to him: 'Father, I have sinned against heaven and against you. I am no longer worthy to be called your son; make me like one of your hired servants.' So, he got up and went to his father."

"But while he was still a long way off, his father saw him and was filled with compassion for him; he ran to his son, threw his

31

arms around him and kissed him. "The son said to him, 'Father, I have sinned against heaven and against you. I am no longer worthy to be called your son.'"

"But the father said to his servants, 'Quick! Bring the best robe and put it on him. Put a ring on his finger and sandals on his feet. Bring the fattened calf and kill it. Let's have a feast and celebrate. For this son of mine was dead and is alive again; he was lost and is found.' So, they began to celebrate."

"Meanwhile, the older son was in the field. When he came near the house, he heard music and dancing. Your brother has come,' he replied, 'and your father has killed the fattened calf because he has him back safe and sound."

"The older brother became angry and refused to go in. So, his father went out and pleaded with him. But he answered his father, 'Look! All these years I've been slaving for you and never disobeyed your orders. Yet you never gave me even a young goat so I could celebrate with my friends. But when this son of yours who has squandered your property with prostitutes comes home, you kill the fattened calf for him!'"

"'My son,' the father said, 'you are always with me, and everything I have is yours. But we had to celebrate and be glad, because this brother of yours was dead and is alive again; he was lost and is found.'"

Notice the great love and affection that the father had, not only for the lost son who came home but also his other son, who became disenchanted and confused. God's love as our Heavenly

Father is unconditional. Even though we may have rebelled and gone astray, His great love is unwavering, as He longs to welcome us back. Even in our selfishness and discontent, as depicted by the older son, He gently and sensibly corrects our actions

Within 1 John 3:1 we read, *"See how great a love the Father has given to us, that we would be called children of God; and in fact we are."* This is so wonderful, so beautiful, so comforting that it must be repeated! Listen to this my brothers and sisters, *"See how great a love the Father has given to us, that we would be called children of God."*

Yes, that is who you are; this is your identity – the son or daughter of the God of this universe! Can it get any better than that? Praise God! 2 Corinthians 1:3 says, *"Blessed be the God and Father of our Lord Jesus Christ, the Father of mercies and God of all comfort."*

Oh friends, but this is just the tip of the iceberg. For God is not only our dear, living and intimate Father, but He is also so much infinitely more than that! The Lord's nature is revealed to us through many descriptive names. Are you ready to learn a few? Here we go!

1. He is Lord, Jehovah, "Yahweh" (Genesis 2:4).
2. He is living God, "Elohim" (Genesis 1:1).
3. He is The Everlasting God!, "El Olam" (Genesis 21:33).
4. He is Lord, Master, "Adonai" (Genesis 15:2).
5. He is The Lord of Hosts, "Jehovah Sabaoth" (1 Samuel 1:3).

6. He is The Most High God, "El Elyon" (Genesis 14:18).

7. He is The Lord God Almighty, "El Shaddai" (Genesis 17:1).

8. He is The Lord My Shepherd, "Jehovah-Raah" (Genesis 48:15, 49:24, Psalm 23:1, 80:1).

9. He is The Lord Our Righteousness, "Jehovah-Tsidkenu" (Jeremiah 23:6, 33:16).

10. He is The Lord My Banner, "Jehovah Nissi" (Exodus 17:15).

11. He is The Lord That Heals, "Jehovah Rapha" (Exodus 15:26).

12. He is The Lord is There, "Jehovah Shammah" (Ezekiel 48:35).

13. He, The Lord Will Provide, "Jehovah Jireh" (Genesis 22:14).

14. He, The Lord Is Peace, "Jehovah Shalom" (Judges 6:24),

15. He is The Lord Who Sanctifies You "Jehovah Mekoddishkem" (Exodus 31:13, Leviticus 20:8).

These are His names, and as Proverbs 18:10 states, *"The name of the Lord is a strong tower; The righteous runs into it and is safe."*

Furthermore, God's attributes are immense and unmeasurable. Here are some of His characteristics.

16. God is Omnipotent – Limitless in His ability to do anything (Colossians 1:6).

17. God is Omniscient – All Knowing (Psalm 147-4-5).

18. God is Omnipresent – Everywhere (Jeremiah 23:24).

19. God is Immutable – Never Changing (Hebrews 13:8).

20. God is Sovereign – Governs over All (Ephesians 1:11).

21. God is Infinite (Psalm 147:5).

22. God is Self-Existent (Psalm 90:2).

23. God is Eternal (Isaiah 40:28).

24. God is the Creator of Heaven and Earth (Psalm 146:6).

25. God is Love (1 John 4:8).

26. God is Wise (Job 12:13).

27. God is Understanding, (Proverbs 3:19).

28. God is Good (Psalm34:8).

29. God is Merciful (Ephesians 2:4).

30. God is Faithful (2 Timothy 2:13).

31. God is Righteous (Psalm 11:7).

32. God is Mighty (Zephaniah 3:17).

33. God is Holy (Isaiah 6:3).

34. God is Just (Luke 18:7).

35. God is Kind (Romans2:4).

36. God is Gracious (Psalm116:5).

37. God is Patient (2 Peter 3:9).

38. God is Compassionate (Psalm 103:8).

39. God is Forgiving (1 John 1:9).

40. God is The Holy Trinity - God the Father, Jesus the Son, and the Holy Spirit; all in One (2 Corinthians 3:14).

Now that we know His names and who He is, His make-up and His attributes, now we get to examine and see what He is in relation to us personally. What comfort and joy we find in discovering who He is to us. Here are few of His limitless attributes.

Yes, He is our Father. Also:

41. He is our Savior (John 3:16).

42. He is our Lord (Psalm 68:19).

43. He is our Comfort (2 Corinthians1:3).

44. He is our Joy (Galatians 5:22).

45. He is our Peace (Galatians 5:22).

46. He is our Shepherd (Psalm 23:1).

47. He is our Guide (Psalm 48:14).

48. He is our Strength (Psalm 28:7).

49. He is our Shield (Psalm 28:7).

50. He is our Refuge (Psalm 91:2).

51. He is our Fortress (Psalm 91:2).

52. He is our Hiding Place (Psalm 32:7).

53. He is our Deliverer (Psalm 18:2).

54. He is our Rock (Psalm 18:2).

55. He is our Protector (2 Thessalonians 3:3).

56. He is our Provider (Philippians 4:19).

57. He is our Friend (John15:15).

58. He is our Wisdom (1 Corinthians 1:30).

59. He is our Hope (Romans 15:13).

60. He is our Life (John 14:6).

61. He is our Redeemer (Isaiah 47:4).

62. He is our Power (2 Peter 1:3).

63. He is our Holiness (1 Corinthians 1:30).

64. He is our Righteousness (1 Corinthians 1:30).

65. He is the Perfecter of our Faith (Hebrews 12:2).

66. He is our Dwelling Place (Psalm 90:1).

67. He is our Sufficiency (2 Corinthians 3:5).

68. He holds us in His hand, and no one can pluck us out of it (John 10:28).

69. He shelters us under His wings (Psalm 91:4).

70. He is the God of all Grace (1 Peter 5:10).

71. He Is the King of Kings and The Lord of Lords (1 Timothy 6:15).

72. He is our Light (Psalm 27:1).

73. He is our Helper (Psalm 54:4).

74. He is our Glory and the Lifter of our Heads (Psalm 3:3).

75. He is the Alpha and Omega, The One Who Was, Who Is and Is to Come (Revelation 1:8).

As a matter of fact, we can go on and on with this list! The marvelous truth is that our identity in God and in Christ is infinite just as He is infinite. Given this tremendously extensive list of God's identities and who we are in Him, is it no wonder that we can confidently say, as did the Apostle Paul, *"If God is for us, who is against us"* (Romans 8:31)?

Isn't this wonderful! This is important to accept since you are made in His image! You are a reflection of Him!! We have as much as we do because of our relationship with God. For this reason, it is no wonder that the prophet Jeremiah declared, *"... 'but let the one who boasts boast about this: that they have the understanding to know me, that I am the LORD, who exercises kindness, justice, and righteousness on earth, for in these I delight,' declares the LORD"* (Jeremiah 9:24, NIV).

As mentioned earlier, we are an extension and a reflection of who God is! Jesus said, *"I am the vine, you are the branches the one who remain in Me, and I in him bears much fruit, for apart from me you can do nothing"* (John 15:5).

God has purchased you. You are His Royal Priesthood, a city set on a hill that gives light to the world. He has given everything He has, and everything He owns. You are an heir of God, created anew in Him, and endowed with His nature, His characteristics, and His power!

In 2 Peter 1:3 we read, *"for His divine power has granted us everything pertaining to life and godliness, through the knowledge of Him who called us by his own glory and excellence."* Dear brothers and sisters, you have it all, the inheritance of His glory!! The critical point is this: that you, *"walk in a manner worthy of the calling with which you have been called"* (Ephesians 4:1).

Your life is a gift given to fulfill your talent in service to others. Abide in Him, and He will abide in You! Live out the gift that God has placed in you!

Jesus said, *"You are the light of the world. A city on a hill cannot be hidden ... Your light must shine before people in such a way that they may see your good works and glorify your Father who is in heaven"* (Matthew 5:14, 16). Here we see that beautiful, powerful word again, "Father!"

38

An observation about light is that it never needs to put any effort into its brightness. Light simply *IS* brightness itself! This is our reality in Christ, that we don't try to be a light, we simply are light, because we abide in Him. Too often the appeal to be Salt and Light may be misunderstood. You will hear believers say something to the effect of, "I want to be Salt and Light in this world or in this situation." The fact of the matter is that you don't have to try dear brothers and sisters, because you abide in Him and He abides in you; let this be a reminder of our main theme, that as Salt and Light to a lost and weary world – your life is a **GIFT**!

Let us live a life that truly reflects our identity as children of God and in a manner worthy of this calling.

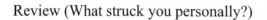

REFLECTION

Review (What struck you personally?)

Revelation (What is God saying to you?)

Response (What are you going to do today)

Chapter 3

Beware of the GIFT Robber

"The thief only comes only to steal and kill and destroy. I came
that they may have life and may have it abundantly."
(John 10:10)

The devil's mission is clear: to steal, and kill, and destroy. His goal is in direct opposition to Jesus, which is for people to live life to the fullest. John 3:16-17 states, *"For God so loved the world, that He gave His only Son, that everyone who believes in Him will not perish but have eternal life. For God did not send the Son into the world to judge the world, but so that the world might be saved through Him."*

Thus, the battle lines between God and Satan have been drawn. God's plan to give you the gift of eternal life, and Satan's plan to keep people from receiving the gift and the destruction of their lives.

The portrayal of our battle is this, *"For our struggle is not against flesh and blood, but against the powers, against the world forces of this darkness, against the spiritual forces of wickedness in the heavenly places"* (Ephesians 6:12).

War strategist expert Sun Tzu said, "If you know the enemy and know yourself, you need not fear the results of a hundred battles."[1]

41

Well, my dear friends, you can be confident of this, that as a believer in Jesus Christ, you will be engaged in hundreds of battles. The battle for your life is a daily reality and a challenge if you are in the army of God. The Apostle Paul stated, *"Just as it is written: 'For your sake we are killed all day long; We were regarded as sheep to be slaughtered'"* (Romans 8:36). That is the enemy's plan.

But hear the exceedingly great news! Verse 37 continues, *"But in all these things we overwhelmingly conqueror through Him who loved us."* God has equipped us and given us the victory!

We need not fear the enemy, for the Bible states, *"You are from God, little children, and have overcome them; because greater is He who is in you than he who is in the world"* (1 John 4:4).

Isn't that beautiful? The battle is not ours, but it belongs to God, and God who is our Father and lives in us is exceedingly greater than the devil in this world.

Listen, friends; we do have the power! Every resource for victory is available to us as believers! There are two fundamental elements that we need to prepare for battle each day:

1. Who is the Enemy, a knowledge of his make-up and strategies?

2. Who are you and the power that you possess in Christ to overcome the schemes of the devil?

Firstly, who is our enemy? As with God our Father and His names, as we discovered in the previous chapter, the enemy carries numerous titles with him. While engaging in battle, we would do well in our preparation to know his identity. Not to fear him but to remain alert in how he portrays himself and his nature.

A few of the devil's titles are as follows:

- In Hebrew, "Abaddon" (Revelation 9:11).
- Accuser of our brothers (Revelation 12:10).
- Adversary (1 Peter 5:8).
- Angel of the bottomless pit (Revelation 9:11).
- In Greek, "Apollyon" (Revelation 9:11).
- Beelzebub, the prince of demons (Matthew 12:24).
- Belial, the personification of all that is evil (2 Corinthians 6:15).
- Coiling serpent, the enemy of the people of God (Isaiah 27:1).
- Dragon (Revelation 20:2).
- Enemy (Matthew 13:39).
- Evil spirit (1 Samuel 16:14).
- Father of lies (John 8:44).
- Great red dragon (Revelation 12:3).
- Leviathan, the symbol of Israel's enemy (Isiah 27:1).
- Liar (John 8:44).
- Lucifer (Isaiah 14:12).
- Lying spirit (1 Kings 22:22).
- Murderer (John 8:44).
- Old serpent (Revelation 12:9).

- Piercing serpent (Isiah 27:1).

- Power of darkness (Colossians 1:13).

- Prince of this world, meaning the world of sin (John 14:30).

- Prince of the devils (Matthew 12:24).

- Prince of the power of the air (Ephesians 2:2).

- Ruler of the darkness of this world (Ephesians 6:12).

- Satan (1 Chronicles 21:1).

- Serpent (Genesis 3:4).

- Spirit that works in the children of disobedience (Ephesians 2:2).

- Tempter (Matthew 4:3).

- The god of this world, a major influence on people living in the flesh (2 Corinthians 4:4).

- Unclean Spirit, meaning wicked (Matthew 12:43).

- Wicked one (Matthew 13:19).

All the names listed point to Satan's evil and cunning character that is hostile towards God and His essence.

Satan's principal character is gross evil, murder, fear, pride, arrogance, chaos, confusion, greed, selfishness, intimidation, hate, perversions, lies, and deception. Every evil that you see in this world originates and is authored by the devil. He is wicked, and there is nothing good that lies in him.

With that in mind, the devil has three primary ways in which he will attempt to trip you up with the ultimate aim of stealing your Gift and destroying you. They are:

1. Your flesh,

2. The world

3. His direct attacks.

1. Your Flesh:

The great evangelist of the 19th century Dwight L. Moody, stated, "I have had more trouble with myself than with any other man I have met."[2] Although, Moody was a powerful influence and a godly man, his greatest struggle was still with himself, that is, his original nature.

The Apostle Paul who God used to write most of books and letters of the New Testament, faced the same struggle. In Romans 7:15-20, he reveals the intensity of this enormous inner battle, when stating: *"For I do not understand what I am doing; for I am not practicing what I want to do, but I do the very thing I hate. However, if I do the very thing I do not want to do, I agree with the Law, that the Law is good. But now, no longer am I the one doing it, but sin that dwells in me. For I know that good does not dwell in me, that is, in my flesh; for the willing is present in me, but the doing of the good is not. For the good that I want, I do not do, but I practice the very evil that I do not want. But if I do the very thing I do not want, I am no longer the one doing it, but sin that dwells in me."*

When you study the lives of every godly man and woman in the Bible and throughout history, you will see that they shared the same battles and challenges, yet they became overcomers through the power of God.

For the truly redeemed one, our time here on earth is not a walk in the park, far from it! It is a fierce battle with ourselves, the world's influences dominated by the devil and his schemes, working in conjunction with our flesh.

In Galatians 5:13-21 we read, *"For you were called to freedom, brothers and sisters; only do not turn your freedom into an opportunity for the flesh, but serve one another through love. For the whole Law is fulfilled in one word, in the statement, You shall love your neighbor as yourself. But if you bite and devour one another, take care that you are not consumed by one another. But I say, walk by the Spirit, and you will not carry out the desire of the flesh. For the desire of the flesh is against the Spirit, and the Spirit against the flesh; for these are in opposition to one another, in order to keep you from doing whatever you want. But if you are led by the Spirit, you are not under the Law. Now the deeds of the flesh are evident, which are: sexual immorality, impurity, indecent behavior, idolatry, witchcraft, hostilities, strife, jealousy, outbursts of anger, selfish ambition, dissensions, factions, envy, drunkenness, carousing, and things like these, of which I forewarn you, just as I have forewarned you, that those who practice such things will not inherit the kingdom of God."*

Here it is, the ugly, sinful elements that characterized our fallen nature. It is hostile and utterly contrary to God.

In Romans 3:10-18, we see the full description of the condition of man's depraved nature:

"There is no one righteous, not even one;

There is no one who understands,

There is no one who seeks out God;

They have all turned aside, together they have become corrupt.

There is no one who does good,

There is not even one.

Their throat is an open grave,

With their tongues they keep deceiving,

The venom of asps is under their lips;

Their mouth is full of cursing and bitterness;

Their feet are swift to shed blood,

Destruction and misery are in their paths,

And they have not known the way of peace.

There is no fear of God before their eyes."

It is no wonder that when John Newton[3] penned the words to the momentous hymn *Amazing Grace*, he wrote, *"Amazing grace, how sweet the sound, that saved a wretch like me."* He did not write "Amazing Grace", *"hat saved a good man like me",* but rather, *"a wretch like me."* Without a shadow of a doubt, John Newton knew the evil condition of his own sinful nature in his appeal to God.

Romans 3:23 reads, *"for all have sinned and fall short of the glory of God."* If good works or adherence to religious activity could save us, we would not need a Savior. However, it is precisely this fallen nature that God came to redeem through the life, death, and resurrection of our Lord Jesus Christ.

47

As with John Newton and the Apostle Paul and all of us who have come to the dim realization of our own unrighteousness before God, we cry out, *"Wretched man that I am! Who will set me free from the body of this death"* (Romans 7:24)?

The answer to this question, the blessed message of the saving Grace of God, is found in the following verse, *"Thanks be to God, through Jesus Christ our Lord"* (Romans 7:25)!

The question then becomes, how do we overcome the flesh so that we might break free from the bondage of our sinful nature and live in the light of His power and goodness? The answer and great paradox in all of this is that it is only in dying to ourselves that we are lifted up with Christ through the power of His resurrection.

The Apostle Paul revealed this great truth when he stated, *"I have been crucified with Christ; and it is no longer I who live, but Christ lives in me; and the life which I now live in the flesh I live by faith in the Son of God, who loved me and gave Himself for me"* (Galatians 2:20).

So how does this work through faith and prayer? A beautiful prayer exemplifying this, written by an anonymous writer, goes: "God, I offer myself to Thee – to build with me and to do with me as Thou wilt. Relieve me of the bondage of self, that I may better do Thy will. Take away my difficulties, that victory over them may bear witness to those I would help of Thy Power, Thy Love, and Thy Way of life. May I do Thy will always!"

Remember the wise and precious words of the prayer of Saint Francis Assis? "For it is in giving that we receive, it is in pardoning that we are pardoned, and in dying, we are born to eternal life. – Amen."

For, "it is in dying that we are born to eternal life." This is the great and blessed paradox! That it is in dying with Christ, as the Bible says, that *"I no longer live, but the Christ lives in me."* Therefore, in that, you awakened to a new life in Christ and empowered to life that reflects His character.

2. The World

The second element that the devil uses is the world and its influences. Jesus identifies Satan as the *"ruler of this world"* (John 14:30). In 1 John 5:19, we read, *"...that the whole world lies in the power if the evil one."*

Additionally, in Job 1:7, *"The Lord said to Satan, 'From where do you come?' Satan answered the Lord, and said, 'From roaming about on the earth, and walking around on it.'"*

The world as we know, at least for now, is the devil's habitat, and it is filled with his presence and every incredible amount of evil. Revelation 12:9 states, *"and the great dragon was thrown down, the serpent of old, he who is called the devil and Satan, who deceives the whole world; he was thrown down to the earth, and his angels were thrown down with him."* This world is his turf; it is his playground where he and his angels roam, taking pleasure in every form of perversity and wickedness.

Furthermore, in 2 Corinthians 4:4, we read, *"... in whose* case *the god of this world has blinded the minds of the unbelieving so that they will not see the light of the gospel of the glory of Christ, who is the image of God."*

Remember, you are a **GIFT**, made in God's **I**mage to **F**ulfill your **T**alent in service to others! Please do not lose sight of this; however, isn't it interesting that *the god of this age has blinded the minds of unbelievers.* Why? So, they can neither see the light, nor experience the light, which is the image of God! That is what the devil is after, to withhold people whom God loves from receiving and accepting the gift.

There is nothing that the devil wants more than to steal and kill and destroy. His objective is to rob people of the light and to do everything in his power to prevent people from receiving and experiencing the 'Gift of Life' that Jesus came to bring.

The forum whereby he conducts his work is right here in this world. 1 John 2:16 reads, *"For all that is in the world, the lust of the flesh and the lust of the eyes and the boastful pride of life, is not the Father's, but is from the worlds"*

We are told *not* to:

1. *"...love the world nor the things in the world..."* (1 John 2:15).

2. *".. don't be conformed to this world, but be transformed by the renewing of your mind, so that you may prove what will of God is, that which is good and acceptable and perfect"* (Romans 12:2).

Realize my beloved brothers and sisters, that this world is not our home, that we are foreigners and exiles in this world. 1 Peter 2:11 urges us in saying,

3. *"Beloved, I urge you as foreigners and strangers, to abstain from fleshly lusts, which wage war against the soul."*

How far and how much ought we to abstain from this world? James 4:4 warns and admonishes those who flirt with the world, *"You adulteresses, don't you know that friendship with the world is hostility toward God? Therefore whoever wants to be a friend of the world anyone makes himself an enemy of God."* You see, beloved, we are *in* this world but not *of* this world.

Before Jesus was to ascend to heaven, he prayed this with regards to His disciples, *"I have given them Your word; and the world hated them because they are not of the world, just as I am not of the world"* (John 17:14).

My dear brothers and sisters, let me reiterate this very important point: we as believers and disciples of Jesus Christ are in this world, but not an active part! That is why we are not to love or be conformed to this world because we do not belong here. The Apostle Paul in Philippians 3:20 states that we are on Earth temporarily, *"For our citizenship is in heaven, from which we also wait for a Savior, the Lord Jesus Christ."*

Now you may ask yourself, if this is not our true home, why doesn't God take us now? After all, this world that the devil and

51

his angels run is no place of comfort for the one who knows and loves God.

It is all foreign to us, for the spirit of this world does not confer with the Spirit of God that abides in us. However, though this world is no comfort to us, God Himself, through the presence of His Holy Spirit, has sent the Comforter to dwell in, serve as a comforter, and to guide us. Furthermore, we have work to do! Just as God sent Jesus into this world, we too have a mission from God. First, we are *God's fellow workers.* 1 Corinthians 3:9 states, *"For we are God's fellow workers; you are God's field, God's building."*

Second, while we are here in this world, we are His Ambassadors. 2 Corinthians 5:20 states, *"Therefore we are ambassadors for Christ, as though God were making an appeal through us."*

Third, Jesus stated in Matthew 5:13-16 that *"you are the salt of the earth; but if the salt has become tasteless, how can it be made salty again? It is no longer good for anything, except to be thrown out and trampled underfoot by people. You are the light of the world. A city set on a hill cannot be hidden; nor do people light a lamp and put it under a basket, but on the lampstand, and it gives light to all who are in the house. Your light must shine before people in such a way that they may see your good works, and glorify your Father who is in heaven"* (Matthew 5:14-16).

Fourth, we are His Messengers! Jesus said, *"And He said to them, 'Go into all the world and preach the gospel to all creation"* (Mark 16:15).

Fifth, we are here to use the variety of gifts and talents God entrusted us with to serve Him and others. In 1 Peter 4:10 we read, *"As each one has received a special gift, employ it in serving one another as good stewards of the multifaceted grace of God."*

With this principle in mind, we cannot forget the Parable of the Bags of Gold which Jesus spoke about in Matthew 25:14-30, and that reflects our calling to be diligent stewards of the gifts and resources that God has entrusted us with. Jesus said:

"For it is just like a man about to go on a journey, who called his own slaves and entrusted his possessions to them. To one he gave five talents, to another, two, and to another, one, each according to his own ability; and he went on his journey. The one who had received the five talents immediately went and did business with them, and earned five more talents. In the same way the one who had received the two talents earned two more. But he who received the one talent went away and dug a hole in the ground, and hid his master's money."

"Now after a long time the master of those slaves came and settled accounts with them. The one who had received the five talents came up and brought five more talents, saying, 'Master, you entrusted five talents to me. See, I have earned five more talents.' His master said to him, 'Well done, good

53

and faithful slave. You were faithful with a few things, I will put you in charge of many things; enter the joy of your master.'"

"Also the one who had received the two talents came up and said, 'Master, you entrusted two talents to me. See, I have earned two more talents.' His master said to him, 'Well done, good and faithful slave. You were faithful with a few things, I will put you in charge of many things; enter the joy of your master.'"

"Now the one who had received the one talent also came up and said, 'Master, I knew you to be a hard man, reaping where you did not sow, and gathering where you did not scatter seed. And I was afraid, so I went away and hid your talent in the ground. See, you still have what is yours.'"

"But his master answered and said to him, 'You worthless, lazy slave! Did you know that I reap where I did not sow, and gather where I did not scatter seed? Then you ought to have put my money in the bank, and on my arrival I would have received my money back with interest. Therefore: take the talent away from him, and give it to the one who has the ten talents.'"

"For to everyone who has, more shall be given, and he will have an abundance; but from the one who does not have, even what he does have shall be taken away. And throw the worthless slave into the outer darkness; in that place there will be weeping and gnashing of teeth."

As temporary as our mission is here on earth, there is much work to be done. Jesus said, *"The harvest indeed is plentiful, but*

54

the laborers are few. Pray therefore that the Lord of the harvest will send out laborers into his harvest" (Matthew 9:37-38).

Will you be the one to accept the call to diligently use your **GIFT** while you are in this world, as His faithful steward? What a day it will be when we finally see Him face-to-face, and He bestows on you the crown life and says, *"Well done, good and faithful servant. You were faithful with a few things, I will put you in charge of many things; enter the joy of your master"* (Matthew 25:21).

Well, what about this world in which we live? Do you want to be free from its entrapments, temptations, and wickedness? The solution and answer to this is beautifully summed up in this hymn written by Helen Howarth Lemmel,[4] it goes like this, "Turn your eyes upon Jesus, look full in His wonderful face, and the things of this world will grow strangely dim in the light of His Power and Grace." So, all we need to do is keep our full attention fixed on Jesus, and He will guide us the rest of the way.

3. Himself, Satan and his angels:

As we have just discovered through our reading, the devil works in conjunction with the Flesh (Man's fallen nature), The World, and thirdly, through direct attacks. In 1 Peter 5:8 we read, *"Be of sober spirit, be on the alert. Your adversary, the devil prowls around like a roaring lion, seeking someone to devour."*

The devil is proud, arrogant, cunning, deceitful, self-centered, perverted, the father of lies and evil to the core. If you want to see a reflection of the devil, look at all the evils in the world from

55

abuse of types, murder, corruption, and utter wickedness. He preys on the poor, the weak, and the vulnerable, and utterly hates God. Everything that God has built, he attempts to destroy, starting from the very beginning of time, in the Garden of Eden, when he appeared as a serpent and planted the seed of sin in the heart of the human race.

Satan is really at war with is God, His divine Angels, and His elect. Those like Simon Peter, whom he desired to sift like wheat, would continue to threaten his destructive mission. The devil is on the attack for those that belong to Jesus Christ. Like a ravenous wolf that sneaks up on the sheep, he seeks and desires to devour the elect. However, as we remain in His loving care, Jesus the Good Shepherd will keep us from the onslaught of the devil and his schemes. Jesus said, *"Peace I leave you, My peace I give you; not as the world gives, Do I give to you. Do not let your hearts be troubled, nor fearful"* (John 14:27).

Speaking to his disciples before His ascension to Heaven, He said this, *"I will pray to the Father, and he will give you another Counselor that may be with you forever"* (John 14:16). This Advocate, this Comforter, this power, this presence is the Holy Spirit, God Himself dwelling in us through His Spirit.

Further in John 14: 26, Jesus reassures us saying,
"But the Helper, the Holy Spirit, whom the Father will send in My name, He will teach you all things, and will remind you of all that I have said to you."

When we believe in Jesus Christ and invite Him into our lives to be our Lord and Savior, something wonderful and powerful occurs. Immediately, we are endowed with the presence of God in our lives through the person of the Holy Spirit, and through His presence in our lives, we become, as Romans 8:37 states, *"... all these things we overwhelmingly conquer through Him who loved us."*

We are given the power to overcome our sinful nature, the world, and all the attacks directed our way from the devil. Yes, we are as scripture declares, *more than conquerors through Him who loved us!*

Listen to what scripture says about your disposition, *"You, are from God, little children, and have overcome them; because greater is He who is in you than he is in the world"* (1 John 4:4). You as a child of God have within you the power to overcome the devil and all schemes. The moment you accept Jesus as your Savior, he is a defeated enemy!

Listen, dear friends, *"... His divine power has granted to us everything pertaining to life and godliness, through the true knowledge of Him who called us by His own glory and excellence"* (2 Peter 1:3).

You have the victory over the devil and all his schemes because the power of Christ lives in and through you!

Brothers and sisters hear the voice of God, *"No weapon that is formed against you will succeed; And you will condemn every tongue that accuses you in judgment. This is the heritage of the*

57

servants of the Lord, And their vindication of me,' declares the Lord" (Isaiah 54:17).

The Apostle Paul in Romans 8:31 affirms this great truth in writing, *"What, then, shall we say about these things? If God is for us, who can be against us?"* and Isaiah 41-10 we read, *"Do not fear, for I am with you; Do not be afraid, for I am your God. I will strengthen you, I will also help you, I will also uphold you with My righteous right hand."*

And if you ever had any doubt of God's power and strength to defend you, hear the words of Jeremiah 20:11 (NIV), *"But the Lord is with me like a powerful champion; Therefore my persecutors will stumble and not prevail. They will be put to great shame because they have failed, An everlasting disgrace that will not be forgotten."*

Throughout Scripture, we can see the might and power of God that overcomes the devil and every form of evil. Therefore, we can unite our hearts in joy and strength and sing from the old hymnal written by Eugene Bartlett[5], "Victory in Jesus! My Savior, Forever!"

We are involved in a war that is far more significant than any other war that has been waged through the centuries. It is a spiritual war fought in the realm's unseen to the eye, but its effects and consequences are still visible and with eternal implications.

The Apostle Paul states, *"Suffer hardship with me, as a good soldier of Christ Jesus,"* (2 Timothy 2:3) and exhorts us in Ephesians 6:10-11, *"Finally, be strong in the Lord and in the strength of His might. Put on the full armor of God, so that you may be able to stand firm against the schemes of the devil."*

Yes, we are at war with the devil, but we have been given the power through Jesus Christ our Lord to overcome!

REFLECTION

Review (What struck you personally?)

Revelation (What is God saying to you?)

Response (What are you going to do today)

Chapter 4

Defenders of the GIFT

"Put on the full armor of God, so that you will be able to stand firm against the schemes of the devil."

(Ephesians 6:11)

If anyone ever told you the Christian life is boring, they are sadly mistaken. If anything, it is filled with excitement, tears, joy, struggle, perseverance, warfare, and victory! Every emotion given to us by God is evoked in this great battle of life, and the most exciting part is the Bible assures us in 2 Peter 1:3-4 the victory in that, *"... His divine power has granted to us everything pertaining to life and godliness, through the true knowledge of Him who called us by His own glory and excellence. Through these He has granted to us His precious and magnificent promises, so that by them you may become partakers of the of the divine nature, having escaped the corruption that is in the world on account of lust."*

We are involved in a tremendous spiritual battle. In Ephesians 6:12, we read, *"For our struggle is not against flesh and blood, but against the rulers, against the powers, against the world forces of this darkness of this age, against the spiritual forces of wickedness in the heavenly places."*

Therefore, with this great reality in mind, we are instructed and provided with a spiritual armor the readies us for battle. In Ephesians 6:13, we read, *"Therefore take up the full armor of God, so that you will be able to resist on the evil day, and have done everything, to stand firm."*

This is *vital, an imperative* for us to defend against the attacks of Satan and his demons. Can you imagine a soldier going into warfare without any equipment, protection, or weapons whatsoever? Chances are he would not last very long, would he?

In the same way, God has provided us with all the weaponry, power, and protection we need for our warfare against the devil, his angels, and devious schemes. His schemes are cunning, baffling, and powerful, and for this reason, we must be alert and fully ready and equipped for battle.

In Ephesians 6:10-18, we read the entire scope of what is needed as we prepare daily for battle: *"Finally, be strong in the Lord and in his mighty power. Put on the full armor of God, so that you can take your stand against the devil's schemes. For our struggle is not against flesh and blood, but against the rulers, against the authorities, against the powers of this dark world and against the spiritual forces of evil in the heavenly realms. Therefore put on the full armor of God, so that when the day of evil comes, you may be able to stand your ground, and after you have done everything, to stand. Stand firm then, with the belt of truth buckled around your waist, with the breastplate of righteousness in place, and with your feet fitted with the readiness that comes from the gospel of peace. In addition to all this, take up the shield of faith, with which you can extinguish all the flaming arrows of the evil one. Take the helmet of salvation and the sword of the Spirit, which is the word of God."*

To recap, we are instructed with six essential elements that complete God's armor and are needed to be armed and ready for spiritual battle.

The Full Armor of God

Put on:

1. The Buckle of Truth, Buckled Around Your Waist
2. The Breastplate of Righteousness
3. Your Feet Fitted, with the Readiness of The Gospel of Peace
4. The Shield of Faith
5. The Helmet of Salvation
6. The Sword of the Spirit, which is the Word of God

In conjunction with putting on the full armor of God, three critical actions are required of us.

1. Be Strong in the Lord and in His Mighty Power!
2. Stand Your Ground, Stand Firm
3. Pray

Even though Christ equips us with all we need for battle, our posture is a posture of defense, in that we are the ones who are being attacked, not the ones on the attack.

We are told to stand firm. The shield of faith is there so that we may extinguish the enemy's fiery darts, and even the sword is implied as a defense mechanism for when the enemy comes face to face with us. But nowhere does it indicate that we ought to go charging into battle.

Could it be that the reason for this is that the battle is not ours, but the Lord's? He is the One who will go on the offensive if need be and at the proper time. In fact, in Revelation 19:11-21, it is revealed that Jesus, upon His second return to earth, will not come as the sacrificial Lamb for the sins of the world as He did the first but will return in great glory as a warrior to defeat Satan!

In verse 11 of Revelation 19, we read the prophetic words of the Apostle John as he writes, *"and I saw heaven opened, and behold, a white horse, and He who sat on it is called Faithful and True, and in righteousness He judges and makes war."*

As we read through the Bible, we see many examples and references of God the warrior defending His own.

In Exodus 15:2-3 (NIV), we read of Moses's song of deliverance, *"The LORD is my strength and my song, And He has become my salvation; This is my God, and I will praise Him; My father's God, and I will praise Him. The LORD is a warrior; The LORD is his name."*

This was made clear when, *"Moses said to the people, 'Do not fear! Stand by and see the salvation of the Lord, which He will perform for you today; for the Egyptians whom you have seen today, you will never see them again, ever. The Lord will fight for you, while you keep silent'"* (Exodus 14:13-14).

Throughout the book of Deuteronomy, we see the same theme exalted. In chapter 3:22, we can hear Moses declaring, *"Do not fear them, for the Lord your God is the one fighting for you."*

In the days of Nehemiah, while God's people were facing adversity and attacks from various people groups, we read, *"At whatever place you hear the sound of the trumpet assemble to us there. Our God will fight for us"* (Nehemiah 4:20)!

In Isaiah is a song of praise that describes God this way, *"The LORD will go out like a warrior, He will stir up His zeal like a man of war. He will shout, indeed, He will raise a war cry. He will prevail against His enemies"* (Isaiah 42:13, NIV).

In Zephaniah, we see the loving heart of this mighty warrior, our God, and our Savior as Zephaniah 3:17 declares, *"The Lord your God is in your midst, A victorious warrior. He will rejoice over you with joy, He will be quiet in His love, He will rejoice over you with shouts of joy."*

Throughout Scripture, we see the mighty hand of God, who protects, rescues, and brings righteousness and justice to those who oppose His loved ones. It is God who fights the battle! In 2 Chronicles 20:15, we read of how the Spirit of the Lord came upon Jahaziel as he spoke the words of the Lord, saying, *"... Listen, all you who of Judah and the inhabitants of Jerusalem, and King Jehoshaphat: This is what the LORD says to you: Do not fear or be dismayed because of this great multitude, for the battle is not yours, but God's."*

If the battle is not ours but the Lord's, what are we to do in the spiritual warfare we encounter? Well, the Bible is evident on this subject. Put on the armor of God! Here it is found within the verses of Ephesians 6:13-14, *"...so that you may be able to resist on the evil day, and having done everything, to stand firm. Stand firm therefore ..."*

We are to stand firm in the faith! Nowhere does it say go on the offense. That is God's call, and He will wage war on our behalf in due time. Meanwhile, our position as soldiers is to firmly stand our ground.

We do not fight fire with fire; in fact, we are instructed to battle evil with good. *Love, joy, peace, forbearance, kindness, goodness, faithfulness, gentleness, and self-control* are the character traits of our battle!

In Romans 12:21, we are told, *"Don't be overcome by evil, but overcome evil with good."* What is interesting to note is that, unlike human wars that are waged by being both on the defense and many times on the offensive, our spiritual warfare, while we await the return of our Lord, is strictly to be defenders of the **GIFT**.

There will be a time when war waged will be led by Jesus and His army as prophesied in Scripture, but the time and season have not yet come. Until then, we are called to put on the full armor of God and stand firm in the faith! In Romans 12:19, we are instructed, *"Don't seek revenge, yourselves, beloved, but give place to God's wrath. For it is written, "Vengeance belongs to me; I will repay, says the Lord."*

Further up in Romans 12:17, we are admonished, *"never pay evil to anyone. Respect what is right in the sight of all people."* In 1 Peter 3:8-9, we are reminded again, *"... loving, compassionate, and humble, not returning evil for evil or insult for insult, but giving a blessing instead."* Finally, if there be any doubt on this issue, we see the same instruction in 1 Thessalonians 5:15, *"See that no one repays another with evil, but always seeks what is good for one another and for all people."*

Our battle is not of rage, strife, anger, and revenge, but love, goodness, self-control, gentleness, and kindness. That is the nature of our conduct in warfare.

Remember what we read in Ephesians 6:12, *"For our struggle is not against flesh and blood."* We are not at war with humanity. Because Satan works through the world to attack God and His ambassadors here on earth, it can lead to the misplacement of our aggression. We are at war with the devil and his spiritual forces. As far as people who do not know God are concerned, this world is full of people who are living under the influence of the devil and need to know the love of God

Jesus not only taught this, He set the example for us time and time again. One of these times accounted for in the Gospels was the betrayal of Jesus in the garden of Gethsemane. As the Roman soldiers under the leadership of the Jewish Religious leaders came to capture Jesus, we read that Peter took out his sword and swung at the servant of the High Priest's head, thus cutting of his ear. What did Jesus do and say? *"But Jesus responded and said, 'Stop! No more of this.' And He touched his ear and healed him"* (Luke 22:51).

It's not that Jesus could not defend Himself and overcome His enemies at the time of His capture; in Matthew 26:53, we read Jesus saying, *"Or do you think that I cannot appeal to My Father, and He will at once put at My disposal more than twelve legions of angels?"* It was not the time or the place to wage war, but rather for prophecy to be fulfilled, just as God had planned as a means to save the world.

As they crucified our Lord, mocking and cursing Him as He hung there dying, what was Jesus' response? *"Father, forgive them; for they do not know what they are doing"* (Luke 23:34). Only love emanated from the heart and lips of Jesus for His enemies.

Jesus' actions in these two dramatic incidences and throughout His entire life were exactly the reflection of what He taught, *"But I say to you, love your enemies, and pray for those who persecute you"* (Matthew 5:44).

There was *no double* standard with Jesus. His words and His life were one of the same. This powerful truth is reinforced in Romans, whereby we read, *"Bless those who persecute you; bless and don't curse"* (Romans 12:14). Furthermore, in Proverbs 25:21, we read, *"If your enemy is hungry, give him food to eat; And if he is thirsty, give him water to drink."*

68

Aside from the fact that this kind of love instilled in our hearts results from our new identity in Christ, it perplexes the world and causes many to inquire about the reason for our faith! Undoubtedly the case when Paul and Silas, as depicted in Acts 16, were delivered from jail by a violent earthquake, and the jailer realizing that the prison doors were open, drew his sword, and just as he was about to kill himself, Paul shouted, *"don't harm yourself! We are all here! The jailer called for lights, rushed in and fell trembling before Paul and Silas. He then brought them out and asked, 'Sirs, what must I do to be saved?' They replied, 'Believe in the Lord Jesus, and you will be saved—you and your household'"* (Acts 16:30-31, NIV).

During great persecution, goodness in action resulted in the Philippian jailer and his household being saved.

Mature Christians conduct themselves, as a result of being filled with the Spirit, in a manner that is entirely contrary to what a person would do in their natural state, at times causing their persecutors to inquire about what makes them who they are. We see this with Jesus as He hung on the cross between two criminals, *"One of the criminals who were hanged there was hurling abuse at Him, saying, 'Are You not the Christ? Save Yourself and us!' But the other responded, and rebuking him, said, 'Do you not even fear God, since you are under the same sentence of condemnation? And we indeed are suffering justly, for we are receiving what we deserve for our crimes; but this man has done nothing wrong.' And he was saying, 'Jesus, remember me when You come into Your* kingdom!' And He said to him, 'Truly I say to you, today you will be with Me in Paradise'"* (Luke 23:39-43).

Right to the end, even as Jesus hung on the cross in unimaginable agony and pain, through His loving grace saved a man even as he himself was dying. It is for this reason that we read in 1 Peter 3:15, *"But sanctify Christ as Lord in your hearts, always being ready to make a defense to everyone who asks you to give an account for the hope that is in you, but with gentleness and respect."* We can go on infinitely throughout Scripture to find examples of how the transforming love of God in our hearts affects others around us and draws them to God.

Now that we have reflected our attitudes and conduct in battle, let's examine the armor of God and what we are to put on as outlined in Ephesians 6.

1. The first is to put on The Belt of Truth (v.14)

Truth is a mighty weapon! When you are girded with truth, nothing can stand against you. It evokes courage, boldness, and strength. With truth, you can look at anybody in the eye and speak with conviction.

It is important to note that the devil is the very opposite of the truth. He is a liar and a deceiver, cunning and manipulative. In John 8:44, Jesus describes the devil as the Father of Lies. When addressing the Pharisees, he says, *"You are of your father the devil, and you want to do the desires of your father. He was a murderer from the beginning and does not stand in the truth*

70

because there is no truth in him. Whenever he tells a lie, he speaks from his own nature, because he is a liar and the father of lies."

That is the very nature of Satan, one who does not hold the truth, for there is no truth in him, and he is the father of lies. The big lie from Satan in the garden of Eden to Eve set the whole world on course towards sin. The devil is cunning and deceitful, and the Bible says, *"No wonder, for even Satan disguises himself as an angel of light"* (2 Corinthians 11:14).

The devil manifests himself in many blatantly wicked ways that are obvious to us. However, his most deceitful schemes have an outer appearance of virtue. Still, inwardly they are just as evil as found in other religions and worldly humanistic philosophies and ideologies.

However, all the lies and deceit that can and will be thrown at you cannot stand against the truth. The truth does not need a defense team or a lawyer. It is strong and pure enough to stand on its own! That is the power of truth! Jesus came to illuminate the world with His truth. Jesus said, *"I have come as a Light into the world, so that no one who believes in Me will remain in darkness"* (John 12:46). We are blessed that Jesus came as light to extinguish the darkness and reveal the ultimate truth.

In John 14:6, Jesus said, *"I am the way, and the truth and the life; no one comes to the Father, except through Me."* Truth is the first line of defense; it is the belt that holds everything else in place. In observing how the Roman soldiers prepared for battle, Paul uses this analogy as instructions for us to buckle our waist

71

with the belt of truth. In essence, he is saying the truth is the centerpiece of your armor. The second part of the armor mentioned is:

2. The Breastplate of Righteousness (v.14)

No soldier at the time would ever think of going into battle without his breastplate. The breastplate was and is essential to protecting the vital organ of the heart. The Bible says, *"Watch over your heart, with all diligence, For from it flow the springs of life"* (Proverbs 4:23).

The righteousness of Jesus Christ is what we are to put on. Furthermore, Jesus said, *"Blessed are those who hunger and thirst for righteousness, for they will be satisfied"* (Matthew 5:6).

Jesus added to this in Matthew 6:33 when stating, *"But seek first His kingdom and His righteousness, and all these things will be provided to you."* Imparted righteousness is the evidence of someone who is continually seeking God!

Suppose a person has claimed to have accepted Jesus Christ in their lives, but there is no change in their lives, no hunger for righteousness, no discomfort with sin, ongoing conformity to the world, and no evidence of the fruit of the Spirit in their lives. In that case, they probably have reason to be concerned about the fruit they are producing in their lives.

Many people self-deceive themselves by thinking that their attendance or activity in "church" or religious activities defines them as Christians. Remember the chilling words of Jesus in Matthew 7:22-23 (NIV), *"Many will say to me on that day, 'Lord,*

Lord, did we not prophesy in your name and in your name drive out demons and, in your name, perform many miracles?' Then I will tell them plainly, 'I never knew you. Away from me, you evildoers!'"

Instead, we would do well to take heed of the words of Micah 6:8, *"He has told you, mortal one, what is good; And what does the Lord require of you, but to do justice, to love kindness, And to walk humbly with your God?"*

Aside from these self-deceived religious prophets and apostates, those who, as 2 Timothy 3:5 says, *"holding to a form of godliness although having denied its power,"* there are also those who like me before my daughter's death claim to be Christians. Still, there is absolutely no evidence of change in their lives, no desire for righteousness and at best, only profess Jesus as their Savior. They are not warriors for God, but those who are self-deceived and headed for a rude awakening when they do have to make an account of their lives before God on that day.

In summary, what are we to do? 1 Timothy 6:11-12 (NIV) puts it very succinctly, *"But you, man of God, flee from all this, and pursue righteousness, godliness, faith, love, endurance and gentleness. Fight the good fight of the faith. Take hold of the eternal life to which you were called when you made your good confession in the presence of many witnesses."*

2 Corinthians 10:4 describes the essence of what it means to put on the breastplate of righteousness! *"... for the weapons of our*

73

warfare are not of the flesh, but divinely powerful for the destruction of fortress."

As we continue our study on putting on the full armor of God, the third component of our protective wear as mentioned in Ephesians 6:15, is to:

3. Fit Our Feet, with the Readiness of The Gospel of Peace

Stu Weber[1], an author and U.S. Army and Green Beret soldier, notes in his book Spirit Warriors that "Historically, far more soldiers on the battlefield have been immobilized by foot problems than have gone down from bullets." Therefore, it would be inconceivable for a soldier to go into battle, fully armed but missing the proper footwear for battle, wouldn't it?

No matter how physically fit a soldier may be, how well-trained and well-equipped he may be if his feet are immobilized, then so is his ability to go to war. For this reason, Paul takes care to note in addressing that the soldier of God needs to have his feet fitted for spiritual battle.

It is also crucial to note that the instruction that we are given in Ephesians 6:13 (NIV) is, *"…to stand your ground, and after you have done everything, to stand."*, and in verse 14, told to *"Stand firm."* If our feet are not equipped with the correct spiritual footwear, then the likelihood that we will slip and fall is probable.

A barefoot soldier will surely encounter debris and harsh landscape during the battle, hindering his ability to defend himself. Like the barefoot soldier, we too can become defenseless, disturbing our peace of mind. So, what causes our peace of mind to become disturbed? The answer is any of the devil's schemes. The devil, during any day, can hurl debris like family feuds, job insecurity, friendship betrayals, or any other rocky situation at us in a way that can disrupt our strength.

Therefore, Paul says, "fit your feet, that comes from the readiness of the Gospel of Peace!" The word "gospel" means "good news," referring to the sacrifice Jesus made for us so that we can be saved. The key concept is to understand that we are at peace with God, which we were given on the day of salvation. When we are at peace, the devil has no power over us!

As a result of the finished work of Jesus Christ through his death and resurrection, the devil is a defeated enemy. He has no power over you, just as he has no power of the Gospel, which is the finished work of Jesus Christ!

These spiritual war shoes are foolproof. With them, you cannot trip, you cannot slip, and you certainly cannot fall! Our feet fitted with the readiness that comes from the Gospel of peace speaks to the firm foundation of our faith, which cannot be moved! It is a positional stance whereby we are in possession of this great truth, God's word!

That devil will do everything he can to throw you off balance, but if you are fitted in the truth of your position in Christ Jesus, you will be able to stand firm! So, as Paul states, brothers and sisters fit your feet with the Gospel of peace so that you may stand firm in battle.

Next, we are instructed to take up the Shield of Faith.

4. Take up the Shield of Faith (v16)

When generally picture a round shield known as a Clipeus, commonly used in ancient warfare when we think of a shield. However, by the time Paul wrote this Epistle, the Roman infantry had developed a highly effective shield that gave them a distinctly superior advantage over their adversaries.

In that day and age, the Roman shield was a unique and powerful part of the soldier's equipment that gave the soldiers a distinct advantage over the opposing forces. This shield that the Apostle Paul referenced in verse 16 was called a scutum, a large rectangular, semi-cylindrical shield. This scutum was made from three sheets of wood glued together and covered with canvas and leather. It varied in size but was commonly 3 to 3.5 feet in length, covering the shoulder down to the top of the knee and approximately 2 to 2.7 feet in width, weighing about 22 pounds. Yet, the scutum was light enough to be held in one hand, and its enormous height and width covered the entire wielder, making it unlikely for him to take a direct hit from flaming arrows.

What does Paul say? *"Take up the shield of faith,* (or what can be called the scutum of faith) *with which you can extinguish all the flaming arrows of the evil."* In essence, the shield of faith, or the "scutum" of faith, protects us spiritually from Satan's fiery darts; in the same manner, a real scutum protected the Romans soldiers physically.

When we take hold of the shield of the faith, the devil and his angels will not be able to wound us by creating doubt, fear, and anxiety in our hearts. Taking up the shield of faith will protect us from withstanding the impact of fiery blows from the devil. Therefore, faith is the bedrock on which we stand. It is an essential and central part of our make-up as believers in Christ.

Scripture declares, *"For by grace you have been saved through faith; and this is not of yourselves, it is the gift of God"* (Ephesians 2:8).

Romans 1:17 reads, *"For in it the righteousness of God is revealed from faith to faith; as it is written: 'But the righteous one will live by faith.'"*

1 John 5:4 says, *"For whoever has been born of God overcomes the world; And this is the victory that has overcome the world; your faith."*

The Bible is full of references to the essential principle of faith. Faith is so much an essential that the Bible says, *"…without faith it is impossible to please God"* (Hebrews 11:6, NIV).

The shield of faith is what will protect you from the schemes of the devil. Therefore, put on the full armor of God and with it, the shield of faith!

5. The Helmet of Salvation (v17)

A Roman soldier would not think of going to battle without his helmet, as it would be pretty foolish. In the same sense, we, too, as Christian soldiers of the cross, need to daily put on our helmet of salvation to protect us from the powerful blow of doubt from the devil.

The helmet in war was designed to protect the head from the weaponry of fiery arrows and long-ended swords measured 3-5 feet in length. Opposing armies would mount their horses with long ended swords and swing them towards the rivals' heads from a distance of 3-5 feet. So, having the helmet on was a vital protective gear.

However, from a biblical standpoint, what exactly is the helmet of salvation? As a Christian, it is vital to realize that our salvation is three-dimensional, in the sense that we are saved, we are being saved, and we will be saved. The helmet of salvation is the confidence and the assurance that the battle is already won, is being won, and will be won.

Jesus, through His death and resurrection, conquered sin and death. At that point, the devil became a defeated enemy. In Hebrews 2:14 we read, *"... since the children share in flesh and blood, He Himself likewise partook of the same, so that through death He destroy the one who has the power of death, that is, the devil."*

As a result of Jesus's death and resurrection, we were presented with the greatest **GIFT** ever, life abundant, free and eternal. *"For we know that since Christ was raised from the dead, he cannot die again; death no longer has mastery over him. The death he died, he died to sin once for all; but the life he lives, he lives to God. In the same way, count yourselves dead to sin but alive to God in Christ Jesus"* (Romans 6:9-11, NIV).

In John 1:12 we read, *"But as many as receive Him, to them He gave the right to become hhildren of God, to those who believe in His name."* As a result of the salvation God gave through the death and resurrection of Jesus and have believed and accepted Him as our Lord and Savior, we became more than conquers in Him. He bore the burden of our sins, conquered death on our behalf so that we may be saved and have the victory.

Then we can say, as the Apostle Paul stated in 1 Corinthians 15:57, *"but thanks be to God, who gives us the victory through our Lord Jesus Christ."*

So, the Apostle Paul is saying here in Ephesians 6:18, put on the victorious helmet of salvation which is already yours because the ultimate battle is already won. Satan and his dominion have no power over you. Jesus has already conquered sin and death on your behalf; victory in Christ Jesus our Savior is already yours!

Know this, if you have repented of your sin, acknowledged, believed, and turned your life over to the care of God, through Christ Jesus your Savior, you have been given the victory! No one can snatch you out of His hands, and there is no condemnation to you who is in Christ Jesus. Your salvation is sealed, and you are safe and secure in Him forever.

Remember, *"No weapon forged against you will prevail, and you will refute every tongue that accuses you. This is the heritage of the servants of the LORD, and this is their vindication from me,"* *declares the LORD"* (Isaiah 54:17, NIV).

79

You may now be asking if we are saved, and the battle is already won, why then are we urged to put on the whole armor of God? Can we not simply bask in our victory? Yes, because of our faith in Jesus Christ, the battle is won. Romans 8:37 states, *"But in all these things, we overwhelmingly conqueror through Him who loved us."*

Yet, there is still warfare going on for the lives and souls of those all around. Remember, the devil roams around like a roaring lion seeking who he may devour. He works daily to plague us with doubts about our salvation and inject the world's desires into our minds so we do not focus on eternity. He is the thief that comes to steal, kill, and destroy.

Though the victory is ours, we are still in battle. The helmet of salvation protects our mind where the devil deals harsh and sometimes fatal blows. There is massive warfare in the invisible heavenly realm for the lives and souls of people who have not been saved. We are the ambassadors and carriers of this great message of hope of salvation to the world.

Then, if you are already saved and secure in Christ, what is the devil's plan of attack, as far as your life is concerned? Well, it is clear and straightforward. He wants to limit your effectiveness as a soldier of the cross so that he limits your effectiveness as bearers of Christ's light to the world. He does this by swiping his two-edged sword made of fear and doubt towards your head in an attempt to make you ineffective.

In numerous cases, he has succeeded in doing just that in his attempt to weigh the Christian soldier down with guilt, fear, and shame. If he keeps you in that mindset, he will have succeeded in limiting your effectiveness. Yet simultaneously, while these are inflicted upon every believer by Satan and his angels, Christ, through the Holy Spirit's work, is continually at work in you to perfect you and make you strong and effective in Him. This process, in theological terms, is called sanctification. It is the ongoing process of God forming you into His image through the power of his Spirit.

Philippians 1:6 declares, *"For I am confident of this very thing, that He who began a good work among you will complete it by the day of Christ Jesus."*

Though we are already saved, our sanctification is an ongoing process. Still, we can rest on this assurance that, *"...His divine power has granted to us everything pertaining to life and godliness, through the true knowledge of Him who called us by His own glory and excellence"* (2 Peter 1:3).

With this, we are encouraged to put on the helmet of salvation along with the whole armor of God so that we may fight the good fight and bring this world out of Satan's grip and into the saving grace of Jesus. We are to be instruments of His work and strengthen God's army by bringing people to the saving knowledge of Jesus Christ, our Savior.

Though we have been saved, there is a day to come when we will be fully completed in Him and will be saved, and ultimate victory will be sealed. Listen to the words of our Lord in Matthew 24:13, *"But the one who endures to the end is the one who will be saved."* Notice the words, *"stand firm,"* indicated in Ephesians 6:14 *"Stand firm then"*, whereby we are to put on the full armor of God.

In James 1:12 we read, *"Blessed is a man who perseveres under trial; for once he has been approved, he will receive the crown of life, which the Lord promised to those who love Him."*

And finally, know this, as we can say with the Apostle Paul, *"I have fought the good fight, I have finished the race, I have kept the faith. Now there is in store for me the crown of righteousness, which the Lord, the righteous Judge, will award to me on that day--and not only to me, but also to all who have longed for his appearing"* (2 Timothy 4:7-8, NIV).

6. The Sword of the Spirit, which is the Word of God. (V17)

Lastly, we are instructed to take up the sixth piece of the armor, the sword of the Spirit, which is the word of God. This is truly exciting, for the sword of The Spirit is where the full power of God is found! There is absolutely nothing that can go against the word of God and succeed. Therefore, it is the ultimate weapon of defense!

Isaiah 54:17 (NIV) states, *"no weapon forged against you will prevail, and you will refute every tongue that accuses you. This is the heritage of the servants of the Lord, and this is their vindication of me,' declares the Lord."*

In Hebrews 4:12 we read, *"For the word of God is living and active, and sharper than any two-edged sword, even penetrating as far as the division of soul and spirit, of both joints and marrow, and able to judge the thoughts and intentions of the heart."*

The sword of the Spirit, the word of God, exposes every lie, refutes every attack, and guarantees every win! The devil will come against you from every direction, but God's word is the ultimate weapon of defense and victory. Isn't it interesting that in Matthew 4:1-11 (NIV), where we read the account of Jesus being tempted by the devil in the wilderness, that He refutes every one of the devil's attempts to lure and detract Jesus from His mission, stating the words affirmatively, "It is written…"

When we visit this passage, we discover: *"Then Jesus was led by the Spirit into the wilderness to be tempted by the devil. After fasting forty days and forty nights, he was hungry. The tempter came to him and said, 'If you are the Son of God, tell these stones to become bread.'*

Jesus answered, 'It is written: 'Man shall not live on bread alone, but on every word that comes from the mouth of God.'

Then the devil took him to the holy city and had him stand on the highest point of the temple. 'If you are the Son of God,' he said, 'throw yourself down. For it is written: He will command his angels concerning you, and they will lift you up in their hands, so that you will not strike your foot against a stone.' Jesus answered him, 'It is also written: 'Do not put the Lord your God to the test.'"

Again, the devil took him to a very high mountain and showed him all the kingdoms of the world and their splendor. 'All this I will give you,' he said, 'if you will bow down and worship me.' Jesus said to him, 'Away from me, Satan! For it is written: 'Worship the Lord your God and serve him only.'

Then the devil left him, and angels came and attended him."

Notice that though Satan tries to tempt Him three times, and each time Jesus pulled out the sword of the Spirit and refuted him by saying, "it is written."

The devil has no power over God's word. The scriptures are the ultimate defense against Satan's tactics, just as it was for Christ in the wilderness.

I so love the word of God, the sword of the Spirit, because within its pages is the answer to every one of life's issues and challenges. It is powerful, accurate, relevant, and nothing can come against it and succeed. Your ability to know and draw from the word of God daily will determine the steadiness of your victorious walk with Christ Jesus.

It is for this reason that we are exhorted in 2 Timothy 2:15 to, *"Be diligent to present yourself approved by God as a worker who does not need to be ashamed, accurately handling the word of truth."*

Listen, the word of God is the very breath of God! It will sustain you through every battle! When the world comes with its temptations and lies, cling to the word of God. When the devil is on the prowl, cling to the word of God, and when flesh attempts to overcome your life, cling to the word God. The Word God will never fail you. *"Your word is a lamp for my feet, and a light for my path"* (Psalm 119:105).

It is for this reason and more that King David exclaimed, *"How I love your law! It is my meditation all the day."* (Psalm 119:97)

In Psalm 19:7-11 (NIV) we see a complete, comprehensive description of the unspeakable value, power and sufficiency found in God's word:

"The law of the LORD is perfect, refreshing the soul.

The statutes of the LORD are trustworthy, making wise the simple.

The precepts of the LORD are right, giving joy to the heart.

The commands of the LORD are radiant, giving light to the eyes.

The fear of the LORD is pure, enduring forever.

The decrees of the LORD are firm, and all of them are righteous.

They are more precious than gold, than much pure gold;

they are sweeter than honey, than honey from the honeycomb.

By them your servant is warned; in keeping them there is great reward."

To summarize, the Word of God is,

- Perfect
- Trustworthy
- Right
- Radiant
- Pure
- Firm

- More precious than gold,
- Sweeter than honey and the honeycomb
- In keeping them, there is great reward!

Dear friends, nothing can stand or come against the word of God. For this reason, we need to make it a top priority to know the word and use it in our daily walk. The sword of the Spirit is your ultimate defensive weapon, and for this reason, scripture encourages us to "always be prepared to make a defense to anyone who asks you for a reason for the hope that is in you." And we do this through the testimony of the living word in us, which is the sword of the Spirit.

The devil aims to do everything within his means to steal, kill and destroy the GIFT within you. However, let's remember that he is already defeated through Christ, and God, through the resource of His armor, has given us all the power we need to stand firm and defend the GIFT He has entrusted us to the end.

With that, as Ephesians 6:11 states, let us, *"Put on the full armor of God, so that you will be able to stand against the schemes of the devil."*

REFLECTION

Review (What struck you personally?)

Revelation (What is God saying to you?)

Response (What are you going to do today)

Chapter 5

Purpose of The GIFT

"...who gave Himself for us to redeem us from every lawless deed, and to purify for Himself a people for His own possession, eager for good deeds."

(Titus 2:14)

Your life is a GIFT! A gift from God to you and a gift from God to others! The gift that God has given you is imperishable, eternal, complete, and meaningful! It is life itself, filled with all the goodness of God. It is designed and shown that you may enjoy life to the fullest, and in doing so, you may glorify your Father, who is in Heaven.

James 1:17-18 states, *"Every good thing given and every perfect gift is from above, coming down from the Father of lights, with whom can be no variation, or shifting shadows. In the exercise of His will He gave us birth by the word of truth, so that we would be a kind of first fruits among His creatures."*

God takes delight in the joy of His children. The Lord loves you and delights in your success and well-being. He is a good God and a loving Father who delights and smiles down at His children! In Zephaniah 3:17 (NIV), *"The Lord your God is with you, the Mighty Warrior who saves. He will take great delight in you; in his love he will no longer rebuke you but will rejoice over you with singing."*

The purpose of God's gift is that you may enjoy it to the full and, in doing so, give Him the glory. The gift of God is wrapped in Good News. So, it is for everyone who believes and receives. In Acts 1:8 we read, *"but you will receive power when the Holy Spirit has come upon you; and you will be My witnesses both in Jerusalem and in all Judea, and Samaria, and as far as the remotest part of the earth."*

And with this divine power, *"… He said to them, 'Go into all the world and preach the gospel to all creation'"* (Mark 16:15).

This indescribable gift of God is not something for us to keep to ourselves, but rather, it is to be presented and shared with the world. This is our mission, and this is our joy!

In Matthew 9:37-38 we read, *"Then he said to his disciples, 'The harvest is plentiful, but the workers are few. Therefore, plead with the Lord of the harvest to send out workers into His harvest.'"*

1 Corinthians 3:9 remind us, *"For we are God's fellow workers; you are God's field, God's building."* and the Apostle Paul reaffirms in 2 Corinthians, 6:1, *"… working together, with Him, we also urge you not to receive the grace of God in vain."*

In other words, we are to be diligent and faithful in the gifts that God has given to us for His service.

Our mission and our calling are to share the glorious news of this wondrous gift of God with others. In that, we are all united in one purpose. With that said, God has given us various gifts specific to us to serve others within His kingdom. In 1 Corinthians 12:4 we read, *"Now there are varieties of gifts, but the same Spirit."*

In a certain sense, that is what makes you unique in your service to God! That is what makes you the gift that you are to others. In 1 Corinthians 7:7, we read that *"...each has his own gift from God, one of this way, an another in that."*

In Romans 12:4-8 (NIV) we read, *"For just as each of us has one body with many members, and these members do not all have the same function, so in Christ we, though many, form one body, and each member belongs to all the others. We have different gifts, according to the grace given to each of us. If your gift is prophesying, then prophesy in accordance with your faith; if it is serving, then serve; if it is teaching, then teach; if it is to encourage, then give encouragement; if it is giving, then give generously; if it is to lead, do it diligently; if it is to show mercy, do it cheerfully."*

It is beautiful to read in Scripture and discover our purpose. But, it is also how we ought to live before God and conduct ourselves with one another. With "one another." That is the key. The original Greek word to describe "one another or each other" in the Bible is "allelon," and it is used 100 times in the New Testament, of which approximately 59 of those references speak to how we should conduct (or not conduct) ourselves with one another.

Our gift, our calling, and specific talents are centered with this purpose in mind. Here is a list of the positive commands to "allelon" one another.

Love one another (John 13:34).

Be devoted to one another (Romans 12:10).

In Give preference to one another (Romans 12:10).

Live in harmony with one another (Romans 12:16, NIV).

Build one another up (Romans 14:19; 1 Thessalonians 5:11).

Be of the same mind with one another (Romans 15:5).

Accept one another (Romans 15:7).

Admonish one another (Romans 15:14).

Greet one another (Romans 16:16).

Care for one another (1 Corinthians 12:25).

Be Serve one another (Galatians 5:13).

Bear one another's burdens (Galatians 6:2).

Forgive one another (Ephesians 4:32).

Be patient with one another (Ephesians 4:2).

Be kind and compassionate to one another (Ephesians 4:32).

Speak to one another with psalms, hymns, and spiritual songs (Ephesians 5:19).

Submit yourself to one another (Ephesians 5:21, NIV).

Consider one another as more important than yourselves (Philippians 2:3).

Look out for the interests of one another (Philippians 2:4).

Bearing with one another (Colossians 3:13).

Teaching one another (Colossians 3:16).

Comfort one another (1 Thessalonians 4:18).

Build one another up (1 Thessalonians 5:11).

Encourage one another (Hebrews 3:13).

Encourage one another in love and good deeds (Hebrews 10:24).

Be hospitable to one another without complaint (1 Peter 4:9).

As each one has received a special gift, employ it in serving one another (1 Peter 4:10).

Clothe yourselves with humility, toward one another (1 Peter 5:5).

Confess your sins to one another (James 5:16).

Pray for one another (James 5:16).

There are also the "how not to treat one another" commands, which are,

Do not lie to one another (Colossians 3:9).

Let's not judge one another (Romans 14:13).

Let's not become boastful, challenging one another, envying one another (Galatians 5:26).

Do not speak against one another (James 4:11).

Do not complain, brothers, against one another (James 5:9).

May we remember, "that a house divided among itself, cannot stand." Moreover, it is essential to remember that discord and strife within the body of Christ are grievous to our Lord and are even considered an abomination. In Proverbs 6:16-19, we read,

"There are six things the LORD hates,

Seven that are an abomination to Him::

haughty eyes, a lying tongue,

93

And hands that shed innocent blood,

A heart that devices wicked plans,

Feet that run rapidly to evil,

A false witness who declares lies,

(and seventh, listen! verse 19)

And one who spreads strife among brothers."

There is no greater family than the Family of God. That is how grave this sin is; it is something God detests. Causing discord in the family of God is a severe offense to Him, one for which He abhors. This is something for which all of us ought to carefully consider before daring to foolishly engage in divisive arguments or discord with other members of the body of Christ. Yet how often, tragically, do we see this among professing believers?

Rather than sin against our Lord in such a grievous way by sowing discord, we ought to write on the tablets of our hearts the supreme teaching of God's Love as stated in 1 Corinthians 13:1-7:

"If I speak with the tongues of mankind and of angels, but do not have love, I have become a noisy gong or a clanging cymbal. If I have the gift of prophecy and know all mysteries and all knowledge, and if I have all faith so as to remove mountains, but do not have love, I am nothing. And if I give away all my possessions to charity, and if I surrender my body so that I may glory, but do not have love, it does me no good."

"Love is patient, love is kind, it is not jealous; love does not brag, it is not arrogant. It does not act disgracefully, it does not seek its own benefit; it is not provoked, does not keep an account of

94

a wrong suffered, it does not rejoice in unrighteousness, but rejoices with the truth; [7] it keeps every confidence, it believes all things, hopes all things, endures all things."

Isn't it interesting to note that of all the one another's mentioned in the Bible, the commandment of Love alone is the most emphasized and referenced at least 16 times throughout the New Testament?

It is no wonder that it is written that the purpose of these "allelon's" is because we are all part of one another. Your needs are my needs and vice versa. We are indivisible, meaning one body bent on one purpose. In a real sense, *"part of one another"* (Romans 12:5; Ephesians 4:25).

16th Century English scholar and poet John Donne[1] eloquently put it in these terms:

"No man is an island entire of itself;

every man is a piece of the continent, a part of the main;

If a clod be washed away by the sea, Europe

is the less, as well as if a promontory were, as

well as any manner of thy friends or of thine

own were;

Any man's death diminishes me,

because I am involved in mankind.

And therefore, never send to know for whom

the bell tolls; it tolls for thee.

Think of it in these terms. We are all part of the body of Christ; when one part of the body hurts, for example, your head, does it affect the rest of your body and your ability to function at your best? This is so with any part of our body; one member of the body inevitably affects another, and so on.

How are we doing with the "one another's"? We all have different gifts, yet we are all bent on one purpose: glorify God and build one another up in the manners described in Scripture.

The 'one another's" have to do with the attitudes we serve and offer our gifts. While the gift has to do with the particular function by which each of us is given a unique role in serving God and one another and ultimately, be the salt and light of the world to which God has positioned us to be.

REFLECTION

Review (What struck you personally?)

Revelation (What is God saying to you?)

Response (What are you going to do today)

Chapter 6

Manifestation of The GIFT

"But to each one is given the manifestation of the Spirit for the

common good."

(1 Corinthians 12:7)

Romans 12:4-6 shares, *"For just as we have many parts in one body and all the body's parts do not have the same function, so we, who are many, are one body in Christ, and individually parts of one another. However, since we have gifts that differ according to the grace given to us, each of us is to use them properly: if prophecy, in proportion to one's faith."*

As a member of the body of Christ, you are separate from the world. You have been redeemed, sanctified, and your life is enriched with the very presence of God Himself, in the form of the Holy Spirit.

Remember, you are endowed with the very nature of God and His characteristics expressed in your life, such as, *"... love, joy, peace, patience, kindness, goodness, faithfulness, gentleness, and self-control"* (Galatians 5:22-23).

Every believer, every member of the family of God, has the Holy Spirit within him; thus, each one of us possesses the fruit of the Spirit. Therefore, we are wonderfully bonded together as one through the presence of the Holy Spirit in each one of our lives.

In that sense, we all share the same spiritual DNA. When a man and a woman come together through marriage and have children, each child is a member of that family, so it is with each of us in relation to our new birth in Christ.

Just as each member of an earthy family shares the same blood flowing through their veins, they are different from one another because each member of the family has their distinct personality, gifts, and abilities. So, likewise, each one of us is given various and specific gifts that define our role in the body of Christ.

At the very least, there are 20 spiritual gifts listed in the Bible and appropriated to various members of the body of Christ, for which each member possesses at least one, and in some cases, several. The gifts which the Bible outlines are:

➢ Preaching	➢ Administrator
➢ Teaching	➢ Evangelism
➢ Encouragement	➢ Apostleship
➢ Giving	➢ Tongues
➢ Helps	➢ Knowledge
➢ Hospitality	➢ Discernment
➢ Mercy	➢ Wisdom
➢ Service	➢ Faith

➢ Leadership ➢ Healing

➢ Pastor ➢ Miracles

Each gift given to us plays a very distinct and essential role in the body of Christ. As Paul indicates in 1 Corinthians 12, although each member of the body is bent on one purpose, not all of us are endowed to function in the same manner but designed to complement and build one another up in Christ through these gifts.

This is how it is so beautiful and explicitly explained by the Apostle Paul:

"Just as a body, though one, has many parts, but all its many parts form one body, so it is with Christ. For we were all baptized by one Spirit so as to form one body—whether Jews or Gentiles, slave or free—and we were all given the one Spirit to drink., Even so the body is not made up of one part but of many. Now if the foot should say, 'Because I am not a hand, I do not belong to the body,' it would not for that reason stop being part of the body. And if the ear should say, 'Because I am not an eye, I do not belong to the body,' it would not for that reason stop being part of the body. If the whole body were an eye, where would the sense of hearing be? If the whole body were an ear, where would the sense of smell be? But in fact, God has placed the parts in the body, every one of them, just as he wanted them to be. If they were all one part, where would the body be? As it is, there are many parts, but one body. The eye cannot say to the hand, 'I don't need you!' And the head cannot say to the feet, 'I don't need you!' On the contrary, those

101

parts of the body that seem to be weaker are indispensable, and the parts that we think are less honorable we treat with special honor. And the parts that are unpresentable are treated with special modesty, while our presentable parts need no special treatment. But God has put the body together, giving greater honor to the parts that lacked it so that there should be no division in the body, but that its parts should have equal concern for each other. If one part suffers, every part suffers with it; if one part is honored, every part rejoices with it. Now you are the body of Christ, and each one of you is a part of it"

(1 Corinthians 12:12-27, NIV).

Now that we have identified the spiritual gifts listed in Scripture, what exactly are the definitions and functions of each one of these gifts? Several types of gifts can be categorized in the following way, although some of them do overlap in terms of their function.

They are the,

1. Communication Gifts
2. Serving Gifts
3. Leading Gifts
4. Outreach Gifts
5. Spiritual Insight Gifts
6. Intercessory Gifts

The Communication Types of Gifts

1. The Gift of Prophecy:

The term prophecy comes from the original Greek word "phemi," which translated means "to speak." Therefore, to have the gift of prophesy means to have the gift of speaking.

The Bible is filled with numerous examples of those who were endowed with the gift of prophecy. As we look to the prophets of the Old Testament, each one of them possessed the gift of prophecy, be it Isaiah, Jeremiah, Ezekiel, Daniel, Hosea, Joel, Micha, Zechariah, Nahum, Jonah, and so many more!

As we look at the life of Jonah, it was this specific gift of prophecy that God gave him to preach the message of repentance to the people of Nineveh. Although Jonah initially ran away from his gift and calling, God still ultimately used Jonah to save the city.

In the New Testament, mainly through the book of Acts, we see many examples of those who preached the word of God with power and authority. In Acts 2, we read the powerful account of the day of Pentecost when Peter stood up and raised his voice to address the crowd. As a result of Peter prophesying that day, Scripture tells us that, *"So then, those who had received his word were baptized; and that day there were added about three thousand souls"* (Acts 2:41).

Prophecy is the gift of speaking prompted by God's word and infused with power by the Holy Spirit! My brother in Christ, Kevin McNulty, is gifted with the ability to speak. I've watched him numerous times simplify the complexity of people problems to groups large and small. Kevin's grasp of human dynamics allows him to impart wisdom in a way people understand, appreciate, value, and apply to improve their personal and professional lives.

In 2 Peter 1:20-21 we read, *"But know this first of all, that no prophecy of Scripture becomes a matter of someone's own interpretation, for no prophecy was ever made by an act of human will, but men moved by the Holy Spirit spoke from God."*

2. The Gift of Teaching:

Most of us can identify rather quickly those that possess the spiritual gift of teaching. Some are entrusted with the ability to articulate and bring to light an understanding of the Bible to others in an effective manner. Who can you identify within the body of Christ that has the gift of teaching? I have learned, grown, and been blessed by teachers such as Allister Begg, Aaron Rogers, David Jeremiah, and Tony Evans, to mention a few of the many brothers in the Lord who have been given this gift.

Of course, as you attend your chosen place of worship, you will indeed find those who serve the body of Christ well with this gift. One such person is Lewis Martin, the pastor of the Madison Church of the Nazarene. I appreciate the sermon series he develops and regularly teaches, allowing us to understand applications of biblical lessons to become more Christ-like quickly.

3. The Gift of Encouragement

The gift of encouragement is derived from the original Greek word "paraklesis," which translates to the term "calling to one's side." It is a unique God-given ability to encourage others in a tremendously effective and remarkable way. Although we are all called in Scripture to encourage one another, we have all seen and experienced individuals in the body of Christ who stand out with a powerfully divine presence to encourage those around them to honor the Lord.

I have personally been blessed by more than a handful of brothers and sisters who have been instrumental in using their God-given gifts to encourage me. One of them is Bob Brumm, "the Encouragement Engineer," and there is a reason he is identified as such. Every time I speak with Bob, he always leaves me feeling encouraged. In the same way, others like my dear sister "The Courage Giver." RJ Jackson also infuses me and so many others with power, genuine and sincere words, and actions of encouragement! These two, Bob Brumm and RJ Jackson, have that wonderful gift of encouragement that makes a profound impact on my life and so many others.

The Serving Types of Gifts

As we are called to serve one another, for this purpose, we will call the following the serving types of gifts. This calls for a personal action or hands-on kind of serving.

4. The Gift of Giving

This gift is possessed by one who gives to others liberally, generously, and cheerfully with absolutely no thought of return. They put others' needs above their own! I know of one such person who possesses this gift is none other than my dear brother in the Lord Frank Marshall, aka "Uncle Frank." I have never seen someone who took such joy in giving than Uncle Frank. He does not simply wait until people ask him for help; he actively searches and looks out for people in need and gives cheerfully, with no expectation of receiving anything in return. I have experienced from Uncle Frank as so many others who know him can testify of the same. For example, one Christmas, Uncle Frank walked into Walmart actively looking for people who may need a helping hand financially and then paying for their items without hesitation. That is the kind of person Frank Marshall is, one who always looks to help and encourage others through giving. What does scripture say about this type of person? Oh, how, *"...God loves a cheerful giver"* (2 Corinthians 9:7)!

Giving is powerful, for it is more blessed to give than to receive, and wonderfully strange enough, it seems that as a child of God, the more one gives, the more one receives! In Proverbs 3:9-10 (NIV) we read, *"Honor the LORD with your wealth, with the first fruits of all your crops; then your barns will be filled to overflowing, and your vats will brim over with new wine."*

A prime example of this powerful principle is none other than the prolific inventor of earthmoving equipment R.G. Letourneau[1], who became unbelievably successful. His many successful ventures supplied 70% of the earthmoving equipment and engineering vehicles used by the allied forces in World War II.

Along with his numerous achievements, he secured 300 patents, built major highways, and even founded a university in Longview, Texas. He was one of the most outstanding business leaders of the 20th century. What was his secret? He made it a habit to give and exercise the gift of giving which God gave him. He discovered that God continued to bless him through his giving, to the point where he ended giving 90% of his personal income and corporate profit to God.

As a result, he did not end up destitute but grew wealthier until his, *"... barns will be filled with plenty, and your vats will overflow with new wine"* (Proverbs 3:10).

5. The Gift of Helping

The gift of help is truly one of the most profoundly meaningful and touching gifts one can possess. The most endearing aspect is that those who have this gift are often "unsung heroes" within the body of Christ, yet so vitally important to its overall function.

The gift of help translated literally means "to relieve, succor, participate in and/or support." It has a broad application and takes on the form of various activities. Those who possess this gift are those we know and see who are always eager to lend a helping hand or provide support in any way needed.

The gift of helping can range from showing courtesy by helping carry luggage for another, opening doors, folding up chairs after a meeting, to making calls on behalf of others and supporting others in the body of Christ through help, prayer, and support.

Often, they are the ones working behind the scenes in support of what may be regarded as the bigger picture. They are such a delight to have around because they eagerly and joyfully find their purpose in helping others accomplish their calling.

Probably very much like yourself, I cannot help but think of those unselfish souls who have made and continue to make my ministerial gifts possible and complete because of their help. Without their support, I would not carry out the dreams and goals God has put in my heart.

For instance, though my name is on it, in writing this book, various contributors have helped make this book possible. Without them, I could not and would not be able to bring this book to fruition.

Often, if not all the time, this gift will show up in the form of a spouse. Without my wife Laura by my side, constantly helping me, I would not accomplish half the things that I venture into. Perhaps it is for this reason that we read in Genesis 2:18 that, in reference to creating Adam, *"Then the LORD said, 'It is not good for the man to be alone; I will make him a helper suitable for him.'"* With that, he created Eve.

Fellow professional speaker and brother in the Lord, Captain Charlie Plumb, tells this story eloquently relayed in an article written by Lee Colan[2] for Inc. Magazine. It is entitled "Who's Packing Your Parachute" and brings home a powerful example of the Gift of Helps in action.

Captain Charles Plumb was a graduate of the Naval Academy. His plane was shot down after 74 successful combat missions over North Vietnam.

He parachuted to safety but was captured, tortured, and spent 2,103 days in a small box-like cell.

After surviving the ordeal, Captain Plumb received the Silver Star, Bronze Star, the Legion of Merit, and two Purple Hearts. Upon his return to America, Charlie spoke to several groups about his experience and how it compared to the challenges of everyday life.

Shortly after coming home, Charlie and his wife were sitting in a restaurant. A man rose from a nearby table, walked over, and said, "You're Plumb! You flew jet fighters in Vietnam from the aircraft carrier Kitty Hawk. You were shot down!"

Surprised that he was recognized, Charlie responded, "How did you know that in the world?" The man replied, "I packed your parachute." Charlie looked up with surprise. The man pumped his hand, gave a thumbs-up, and said, "I guess it worked!"

Charlie stood to shake the man's hand and assured him, "It most certainly did work. If it had not worked, I would not be here today."

Charlie could not sleep that night, thinking about the man. He wondered if he might have seen him and not even said, "Good morning, how are you?" He thought of the many hours the sailor had spent bending over a long wooden table in the bottom of the ship, carefully folding the silks and weaving the shrouds of each chute, each time holding in his hands the fate of someone he didn't know.

Plumb then realized that he needed mental, emotional, and spiritual parachutes along with the physical parachute. He had called on all these supports during his long and painful ordeal.

How often do you miss the opportunity to thank those people in your organization who are "packing your parachute?

As leaders or teachers, it is essential to realize that we do not work on our own. Instead, God has gifted people to come alongside us to assist in ways that will enable us to achieve and complete God's calling.

As with Captain Charlie Plumb's parachute packer, we too have parachute packers in our lives that possess the spiritual gift of help so that our calling in life may be complete.

6. The Gift of Hospitality

Just imagine a world without hospitality. For a few examples, restaurants, hotels, travel, recreational services, tourism, and event planners would probably look almost unrecognizable without the demonstration and implementation of hospitality services, etc. It is a crucial part of the customer service industry, and for those corporations which rely on it heavily, they tend to do exceedingly well; there is great reward and joy for both the customer and those who render these services.

But as with all spiritual gifts, the gifts mentioned in Scripture have a higher and deeper meaning that stems from completely pure and unselfish motives.

In its original Greek, the word hospitality in the Bible is "philoxenia," which directly translated as "love of strangers." It is an extension of godly hospitality that seeks to provide comfort and pleasantry to others without any motive for financial compensation. It pours out of a heart of love for others.

Near my home, there is a wonderful brother in the Lord by the name of Robert Summerford. He is known for opening his home and facility to others that they may experience the love of God. It pours out of a pure heart and brings joy and encouragement to those around.

Those with the spiritual gift of hospitality are those we may find at the front door of their church warmly welcoming people into the fellowship. It may also be those who are keenly tuned in to others and always looking for ways to have people feel loved and accepted. It sometimes may be in the simple form of offering food and beverage and being welcoming and thoughtful to introduce newcomers to others. It takes many forms, yet it flows out of a keen spiritual awareness of others.

7. The Gift of Mercy

The spiritual gift of mercy expresses itself through sensitivity and compassion towards those who are less privileged and are suffering in any way, be it physically, mentally, emotionally, financially, and spiritually.

For example, those involved in providing shelter, food, and special needs to the homeless, visiting the sick and the elderly, giving hope and comfort for those incarcerated or in an addiction recovery home often do so because of the gift of mercy God gave them. These individuals are naturally on the lookout and readily

111

available to help, serve and show compassion for those in distress or are suffering.

The characteristics of those endowed with this gift of mercy are demonstrated through an extraordinary expression of love, kindness, gentleness, compassion, sensitivity, understanding, sympathy, humility, and self-sacrifice. They weep with those who mourn, rejoice with those who rejoice, and ultimately pour out their lives as a gift offering to others.

Perhaps one of the most vivid examples of mercy in action is found in the parable of the Good Samaritan found in the Gospel of Luke 10:30-35 (NIV):

"In reply Jesus said: 'A man was going down from Jerusalem to Jericho, when he was attacked by robbers. They stripped him of his clothes, beat him and went away, leaving him half dead. A priest happened to be going down the same road, and when he saw the man, he passed by on the other side. So too, a Levite, when he came to the place and saw him, passed by on the other side.'"

"'But a Samaritan, as he traveled, came where the man was; and when he saw him, he took pity on him. He went to him and bandaged his wounds, pouring on oil and wine. Then he put the man on his own donkey, brought him to an inn and took care of him. The next day he took out two denarii and gave them to the innkeeper. 'Look after him,' he said, 'and when I return, I will reimburse you for any extra expense you may have.'"

So many insights and lessons can be drawn from this well-known and powerful parable, as many scholars have done over the years. But if there is one thing for sure, it is a beautiful and profoundly touching account of the gift of mercy.

8. The Gift of Service

The spiritual gift of service often refers to those who are in love with volunteering their time, resources, and talents to others for the sake of building up the body of Christ.

For several years now, I've had the joy and blessing of collaborating with the wonderful faith-based organization, the Link of Cullman. If there was any organization or group of individuals who, in my viewpoint, exemplify the gift of service, it is these loving souls.

As with those at the Link of Cullman and other organizations alike around the world, the driving force behind it all is an ever-present eagerness to serve others! Moreover, the gift of service is a direct reflection of the calling Jesus placed on His disciples and the measure of greatness in the kingdom of God.

We see this in Matthew 20:25-28, whereby, *"But Jesus called them to Himself and said, "You know that the rulers of the Gentiles domineer over them, and those in high position exercise authority over them. It is not this way among you, but whoever wants to become prominent among you shall be your servant, and whoever desires to be first among you shall be your slave; just as the Son of Man did not come to be served, but to serve, and to give His life as a ransom for many."*

Jesus exemplified the attitude of service in John 13:12-15 where we read the account of Jesus the God of heaven and earth

113

reaching down to wash the feet of His disciples, *"Then, when He had washed their feet, and taken His garments and reclined at the table again, He said to them, 'Do you know what I have done for you?' You call Me 'Teacher' and 'Lord'; and [a]you are correct, for so I am. So, if I, the Lord and the Teacher, washed your feet, you also ought to wash one another's feet. For I gave you an example, so that you also would do just as I did for you."*

Now, if Jesus, who is God, washed the feet of His disciples, how much more might we do for others as a gift of service to them?

The Leading Types of Gifts

God has gifted some to communicate His Word. In addition, they are anointed with special gifts of service and others to lead them. Here we will look at the leading types of spiritual gifts, which include the following.

9. The Gift of Leadership

The gift of leadership is appointed to those whom God has given a clear vision and mission. The people given this tremendous gift are equipped with the ability to share the vision and mission to those they serve in a manner that gains the practical cooperation of others.

The greatest example of the gift of leadership in the Bible is none other than Jesus Himself. Notably, Jesus's form of leadership is unlike that which we see in the world. His leadership is filled with compassion and deep care for the well-being of those He serves. Jesus is consumed with serving others rather than telling

114

and expecting others to follow. As indicated in Mark 9:35, *"And sitting down, He called the twelve and he said to them, 'If any man wants to be first, he shall be the last of all, and servant of all.'"*

The ones bestowed with this gift do not seek to be served but rather are consumed with caring and serving those whom he has been entrusted with to lead. In Proverbs 27:23 we read, *"Know well the condition of your flocks, And pay attention to your herds,"* and that is exactly how one who has been entrusted with this enormous gift should work.

Church planters, evangelists, and pastors are often given roles whereby we can see the gift of leadership on display.

Other examples of biblical figures to observe and learn and draw from in terms of being given the gift of leadership are godly individuals such as Abraham, Moses, Joshua, Gideon, King David, King Solomon, the prophets, and all of Jesus's disciples.

10. The Gift of Pastor

Infused in the gift of the Pastor is leadership, yet not all who possess the gift of leadership have a pastoral gift. The gift of a pastor is expressed through the responsibility of guiding, protecting, and feeding a group of believers entrusted to his care. Just as a shepherd cares for his sheep as depicted in scripture, so a pastor is a shepherd who diligently attends to the cares and needs of those who he has been called to serve.

The Apostle Paul listed some of the qualifications of a Pastor in Titus 1:7-9 (NIV). *"Since an overseer manages God's household, he must be blameless—not overbearing, not quick-*

115

tempered, not given to drunkenness, not violent, not pursuing dishonest gain. Rather, he must be hospitable, one who loves what is good, who is self-controlled, upright, holy and disciplined. He must hold firmly to the trustworthy message as it has been taught, so that he can encourage others by sound doctrine and refute those who oppose it."

Once again, just as with the gift of leadership, the gift of being a pastor is best exemplified in the way Jesus loved and cared for others, particularly His disciples. Jesus said in John 10:11, *"I am the good shepherd; the good shepherd lays down His life for the sheep."*

11. The Gift of Administration

In the original Greek, the gift of administration is "kubernesis," which translated as "to steer." It is a specific term that was often used to describe a shipmaster or captain. The gift of administration is a type of leadership gift that provides one with the spiritual ability to effectively steer the body toward achieving God-given visions and goals by planning, organizing, and providing supportive resources to those they serve. This gift can range from financial administration to administrating the plans, goals, and activities of those who serve as various parts of what makes up the body of Christ.

When I think of the gift of administration, Ms. Carol Brigance comes to the top of my mind. She attended the First Baptist Church of Huntsville, Alabama, and was continuously asked to support various committees due to her administration skills of accuracy, precision, and attention to detail. Her ability in organizing training management programs led to her selection to direct several high-visibility projects for work.

The Outreach Types of Gifts

God has given spiritual gifts for the equipping, health, and inner growth of the Church and the growth of the Body through reaching out to those who do not know Him. Spiritual Gifts that are most used for outreach include:

12. The Gift of Evangelism

As followers of Christ, we are called to share the good news of the Gospel, and some are given more responsibility in this area. The Greek word for "evangelist" is "Euaggelistes" which means "one who brings good news." They are burdened for the lost and take every opportunity to introduce others to the saving knowledge of Jesus Christ.

This comes in everyday interactions with others and is also a gift that can be combined with the gift of prophecy, where it is spoken out to the masses. As it was with men of God such as Billy Graham in the 20th century, Dwight L. Moody in the 19th, going back to the apostle Paul and Peter, who notably spoke out in the power of God on the day of Pentecost, when 3,000 people were saved and added to the church.

13. The Gift of Apostle

It is helpful to distinguish the difference between the term "the office of apostleship" versus "the gift of apostle." According to scripture, the *office of apostleship* was reserved for those who

117

walked and talked with Jesus first-hand and were given direct instruction by Him during His physical time on earth, as well as becoming His vessels through which to write the New Testament. All of Jesus' twelve disciples were apostles and Paul, who had a direct encounter with Christ on the road to Damascus and was instrumental in writing much of the New Testament, as the Word of God was breathed out through him by the Holy Spirit. These men were what we identify as the original Apostles.

The gift of apostleship still lives on as the original Greek term defines it as, "apóstolos" which means "one who is sent off." Thus, it refers to those who have explicitly been sent out or ordained with a specific mission.

Those blessed with apostleship have many different abilities = to carry out the mission for which they have been called. They can be identified as leaders of leaders and ministers of ministers. They are visionaries and influencers. Often missionaries, church planters, senior pastors, and those leading multiple ministries or churches have been equipped with the gift of apostleship bestowed on them by God.

They can be identified as leaders marked by exceptional humility, godliness, wisdom, and service to others. As indicated in Mark 9:35, *"And sitting down, He called the twelve and said to them, 'If anyone who wants to be first, he shall be last of all and the servant of all.'"*

From the Church of the Firstborn Ministries in Cottondale, Alabama, Darryl Jackson has the gift of apostleship. He continues to plant new ministries and churches, go into places where the Gospel is not preached, and reach across cultures to establish churches in challenging environments and raise up and develop leaders throughout the United States and abroad.

They often have many different gifts that allow them to fulfill their ministry. This demeanor that encompasses the gift of apostleship is found throughout the book of Acts and particularly brought to light in 1 Thessalonians, 2:1-12 (NIV), where Paul, Silas, and Timothy give an account of their testimony and the gift of apostleship: *"You know, brothers and sisters, that our visit to you was not without results. We had previously suffered and been treated outrageously in Philippi, as you know, but with the help of our God we dared to tell you his gospel in the face of strong opposition. For the appeal we make does not spring from error or impure motives, nor are we trying to trick you. On the contrary, we speak as those approved by God to be entrusted with the gospel. We are not trying to please people but God, who tests our hearts. You know we never used flattery, nor did we put on a mask to cover up greed—God is our witness. We were not looking for praise from people, not from you or anyone else, even though as apostles of Christ we could have asserted our authority. Instead, we were like young children among you."*

"Just as a nursing mother cares for her children, so we cared for you. Because we loved you so much, we were delighted to share with you not only the gospel of God but our lives as well. Surely you remember, brothers and sisters, our toil and hardship; we

worked night and day in order not to be a burden to anyone while we preached the gospel of God to you. You are witnesses, and so is God, of how holy, righteous and blameless we were among you who believed. For you know that we dealt with each of you as a father deals with his own children, encouraging, comforting and urging you to live lives worthy of God, who calls you into his kingdom and glory."

14. Gift of Tongues

The Bible reveals two different uses for the gift of tongues. One is for self-edification. In 1 Corinthians 14:2 we read, *"For the one who speaks in a tongue does not speak to people, but to God; for no one understands, but his spirit he speaks mysteries"* This is referred to as the speaking of tongues used in prayer to God to build and strengthen the one in private devotional prayer to God. The other use of what is more widely regarded as the gift of tongues is to glorify God and build up the Church.

This is spoken in a different language that is unknown to the one who is speaking it but meant to communicate the word from God in a divine orderly fashion to those others, *"so that the church may be edified"* (1 Corinthians 14:5, NIV) and accompanied by an interpreter as indicated in verse 7, *(should speak, one at a time, and someone must interpret)*.

The Insight Types of Gifts

The insight gifts are provided so that those in the body of Christ may be able to be guarded against destructive lies and protected from falsehood. To provide insights that enable believers to discern right from wrong, truth from falsehood. To gain wisdom, discretion, and guidance leads to a clear understanding of the truth and every good and correct course of action.

15. Gift of Knowledge

The gift of knowledge is given ultimately to build up the body of Christ. It demonstrates itself in the form of a wonderfully deep and exceptional understanding of God's Word, which brings joy, enlightenment, and encouragement to others! Those who have the gift of knowledge have been given a beautiful ability to understand and unveil the truths of God's word, often in a timely fashion, with soundness of mind, clarity, and precision.

You can identify one who has the gift of knowledge, by his absolute thirst and love for God's Word, which he pursues relentlessly. In Psalm 119:97, we read David extolling his desire for knowledge, *"How I love your law! It is my meditation all day."*, and likewise in Psalm 42:1, he cries out, *"As the deer pants for the water brooks, So my soul pants for You, God."*

In the letter to the Philippians, the Apostle Paul's firmly states his primary pursuit, *"What is more, I consider everything a loss because of the surpassing worth of knowing Christ Jesus my Lord, for whose sake I have lost all things. I consider them garbage, that I may gain Christ"* (Philippians 3:8, NIV).

Why is this? Paul explains in 1 Corinthians 1:5, *"that in everything you were enriched in Him, in all speech and all knowledge."*

121

The gift of knowledge stems from the pursuit of knowing Christ. It begins and is marked by a sincere desire to know God, and that desire is internalized and powerfully translated into the gift of knowledge.

One who has the gift of knowledge can see everyday circumstances and current events through the lenses of Scripture. Moreover, knowledge and understanding God's ways are deeply embedded in their hearts, committed to memory. Thus, they often roll off their lips as the Spirit moves to address situations appropriately.

Have you ever heard of a person being described as a "walking Bible?" That person is likely endowed with the gift of knowledge. Likewise, many who are drawn to further their education through theological studies and become teachers and pastors are also likely to be blessed with the gift of knowledge to build up the body of Christ in the knowledge of our Lord.

An outstanding example of the gift of understanding is my dear friend, Phil Taylor. He served as my advisor in the writing of *You Are A GIFT*. His profound insights into the meaning of scriptures to understand all the Father has revealed in His word.

16. Gift of Discernment

One of the significant challenges that we experience as we walk with the Lord is that the devil is always on the move, doing all he can to steal, kill, and destroy us. He seeks to deter you from your walk with Him so that your effectiveness in utilizing your God-given gifts is stifled.

122

For this reason, we must remain diligent in holding onto the Word of Truth as our anchor for life. 2 Timothy 2:15 says, *"Be diligent to present yourself approved to God as a worker who does not need to be ashamed, accurately handling the word of truth."*

We are to be committed to the quest for truth as the Bereans were, mentioned in Acts 17:11, *"... for they received the word with great eagerness, examining the Scriptures daily to see whether these things were so."* As with the Bereans, if we are to be wise, we ought to do the same.

Religious airwaves, educational institutions, and this world are jammed packed with false teachers, who are under the coordination and spell of the devil, the Father of Lies.

In John 8:44, Jesus describes the devil in these terms, *"...He was a murderer from the beginning, and does not stand in the truth because there is no truth in him. Whenever he tells a lie, he speaks from his own nature, because he is a liar and the father of lies."*

He lied in the garden and continues his works of deception to this day. He launches and conducts his devious schemes through teachers who present themselves as sheep but are ravenous as wolves. Jesus warns us in Matthew 7:15 to *"Beware of false prophets, who come to you in sheep's clothing, but inwardly are ravenous wolves."*

As with all the other gifts listed, you can write an entire book on just this topic alone. Scripture is filled with godly warning and pleas to be on the alert and stay clear of false teachers and evil influencers.

For instance, Jesus warns us in Matthew 24:11, *"And many false prophets will rise up and mislead many astray."*

The Apostle John warns, *"Beloved do not believe every spirit, but test the spirits, to see whether they are from God, because many false prophets have gone out into the world"* (1 John 4:1).

Paul states, *"For such people are false apostles, deceitful workers, masquerading as apostles of Christ. And no wonder, for Satan himself masquerades as an angel of light. It is not surprising, then, if his servants also masquerade as servants of righteousness. Their end will be what their actions deserve"* (2 Corinthians 11: 13-15, NIV).

2 Timothy 4:3 declares, *"For the time will come when they will not tolerate sound doctrine; but, wanting to have their ears tickled, they will accumulate for themselves teachers in accordance with their own desires."*

If that is not enough to convince us of the urgency and danger of false teachers, Peter adds, *"But there were also false prophets among the people, just as there will be false teachers among you. They will secretly introduce destructive heresies, even denying the sovereign Lord who bought them--bringing swift destruction on themselves"* (2 Peter 2:1, NIV). These warnings are just a fragment of this force of deception that is at work in this world today!

If there were not such an onslaught of false teachings and epidemic of false teachers, there would not be such a great need for those with the gift of discernment, but as we can clearly see, as mentioned in Scripture, there is! Therefore, we must choose to be on guard, and for this reason, God has raised leaders in the body of Christ with the gift of discernment to serve and protect the elect and direct us to the truth.

The Apostle Peter provides an excellent example of discernment. In Acts 5:1-1, he discerned Ananias was lying to him when he and his wife Sapphira told him that they had sold land and were donating all the proceeds of the land to the church. But Peter knew they were both lying. How did he know? He had been given the gift of discernment and was able to see through to their true nature and knew immediately that their motives were evil.

17. Gift of Wisdom

The gift of wisdom is the spiritual ability to discern and respond to any circumstance in a right, just, and fair manner. The insight, knowledge, and godly confidence to take every good course in every set of circumstances life presents. The Biblical use of the word wisdom is for us to make scriptural truths relevant and practical in everyday living and decision-making. The result is Godly insight which allows us to exercise sound judgment.

The gift of wisdom is so special, valuable, and unique from the other gifts of the Spirit that in studying God's Word, it is revealed as perhaps the only gift which every believer has at their disposal. Yet, not all believers put it to use. Though it is available to all believers, only those who seek it diligently and ask for it receive it. This is the difference between those who experience it and those who do not.

1 Corinthians 1:30 states that, *"But it is due to Him that you are in Christ Jesus, who became to us wisdom from God, and righteousness and sanctification, and redemption."*

In James 1:5 we read, *"But if any of you lacks wisdom, let him ask of God, who gives to all generously and without reproach, and it will be given to him."*

In a sense, the gift of wisdom is unique from other gifts in that it can be likened to the fruit of the Spirit, which is available to all. The gift of wisdom is such that it is manifested in the following way. *"But the wisdom from above is first pure, then peace-loving, gentle, reasonable, full of mercy and good fruits, impartial, free of hypocrisy"* (James 3:17).

So, if the activation of the gift of wisdom is available to all believers, then why is it identified as a gift of the spirit and not overwhelmingly evident in the lives of all believers? As indicated in the Book of James, the answer is simple: You do not have because you do not ask God.

In 1 Chronicles 1:7-12, 3:5-15 (NIV), we read a powerful account of one who was keenly aware of his need for wisdom and how God blessed and answered Solomon's earnest desire and request. *"That night God appeared to Solomon and said to him, 'Ask for whatever you want me to give you.' Solomon answered God, 'You have shown great kindness to David my father and have made me king in his place. Now, LORD God, let your promise to my father David be confirmed, for you have made me king over a people who are as numerous as the dust of the earth. Give me*

126

wisdom and knowledge, that I may lead this people, for who is able
to govern this great people of yours?'

God said to Solomon, 'Since this is your heart's desire and
you have not asked for wealth, possessions or honor, nor for the
death of your enemies, and since you have not asked for a long life
but for wisdom and knowledge to govern my people *over whom I*
have made you king, therefore wisdom and knowledge will be
given you. And I will also give you wealth, possessions and
honor, such as no king who was before you ever had and none
after you will have.'"

The gift of God's wisdom was afforded to Solomon, but why?
We see that it was because King Solomon earnestly desired and
asked for it! As it was with King Solomon, so it is with each one of
us. God is always before us extending His grace, saying, *"But if*
any of you lacks wisdom, let him ask of God, who gives to all
generously and without reproach, and it will be given to him"
(James 1:5).

1 Corinthians 12:31 states, *"But earnestly desire the greater*
gifts. And yet, I am going to show you a far better way." With that
said, how and where does wisdom rank in terms of its greatness?

Proverbs 4:7 affirms it in this way, *"... Acquire wisdom; And*
with all your possessions, acquire understanding." Throughout the
entire book of Proverbs and scripture, we read of the unspeakable
value found in obtaining wisdom.

Proverbs 3:13-18 (NIV) sums up the unmeasurable greatest of
wisdom this manner:

127

"Blessed are those who find wisdom,

those who gain understanding,

for she is more profitable than silver

and yields better returns than gold.

She is more precious than rubies;

nothing you desire can compare with her.

Long life is in her right hand;

in her left hand are riches and honor.

Her ways are pleasant ways,

and all her paths are peace.

She is a tree of life to those who take hold of her;

those who hold her fast will be blessed."

My Christian mentor, Brian Gable, possesses the gift of wisdom. He loves to read, meditate, and commune with God, drawing wisdom that applies the scriptures to everyday living. Brian shared how he has applied Proverbs 29:23, *"A person's pride will bring him low, But a humble spirit will obtain honor"* to make a life decision. In this season of his life, he recognized the need to forgo an opportunity knowing God would reward him for standing firm in his faith.

The Intercessory Types of Gifts

Within the Church, we need people who believe God can move mountains and do that which is seemingly impossible. These people spur others to trust God for great things, often taking us out of our comfort zones and shaking up our status quo. They usually have one of the following gifts.

128

18. Gift of Faith

All believers in the Lord Jesus Christ have come to Him because of saving faith. All Christians possess a saving faith, but not all have received what is defined in scripture as the Gift of Faith.

The gift of faith is an extra measure of faith given to those who are firmly persuaded of God's power and promises to accomplish His will and purpose. It is a display of confidence in God and His Word that no circumstance or obstacles will shake that conviction.

In discussion with my good friend Phil Taylor, he shared how his mother would continually speak words of Godly assurance and faith into his life during his childhood. The expression of her words stemmed directly from the gift of faith given to her to assure comfort and encouragement. Phil shared that as she spoke, she did so with a beautiful and utter conviction of faith which left no room for doubt, and sure enough, the expression of her Godly gift of faith would produce the positive result of that conviction. As Phil explained, Mrs. Marguerite Taylor did not only use this gift to edify and build him up but that he bore witness to the expression of that gift of faith in her life. She used it accordingly and on time with so many others throughout her life, including Fernand Saint Louis.

Mrs. Taylor, through her faith, was the wonderful instrumental GIFT from GOD that propelled Fernand to receive his call to full-time ministry in 1963 as a radio and television evangelist.

Do you know people like that? Who do you know that has this type of faith, that when they speak or pray, is moved by an extraordinary and overwhelming conviction that what God has spoken through His Word and through that person's heart will come to pass?

As my friend Phil shared, his mother had both the gift of encouragement and the gift of faith combined, and when implemented, it became a powerful combination!

19. Gift of Healing

As described in 1 Corinthians 12:9, 28, 30, the gift of healing is manifested as a means through which God makes people whole either physically, emotionally, mentally, or spiritually.

In James 5:14-15 (NIV), we read, *"Is anyone among you sick? Let them call the elders of the church to pray over them and anoint them with oil in the name of the Lord. And the prayer offered in faith will make the sick person well; the Lord will raise them up. If they have sinned, they will be forgiven."*

The gift of healing is alive and well today, just as it has always been, and as indicated in 1 Corinthians 12:11, *"But one and the same Spirit works all these things, distributing to each one individually just as He wills."* As with all the other gifts, the focus ought not to be on the person bearing the gift but on the source of the gift itself, The Lord Jesus Christ.

The Apostle Paul, as with several other of Christ's disciples, had the gift of healing. In Acts 28:8 (NIV), we read the account of the father of Publius and how the Spirit healed him through the touch of Paul's hands, *"His father was sick in bed, suffering from fever and dysentery. Paul went in to see him and, after prayer, placed his hands on him and healed him."*

In Mark 6:12-13, we read, *"And they went out and [a]preached that people are to repent. And they were casting out many demons and were anointing with oil many sick people and healing them."*

Throughout Scripture, we read account after account of those healed because of the gift of healing bestowed on the disciples. And so, as it was before and after the day of Pentecost, the gift of healing is distributed as God wills to be performed for the collective benefit of the body of Christ.

20. Gift of Miracles

The spiritual gift of miracles is described in Scripture much like the gift of healing. It is found in 1 Corinthians 12:10. The original Greek phrase "energemata dynameon" literally translates as "workings of powers."

Jesus, the ultimate miracle worker, multiplied fish and loaves of bread, walked on water, raised the dead, turned water into wine, and performed many miracle healings. He said this to His disciples, *"Truly, truly I say to you, the one who believes in Me, the works that I do, he will do also; and greater works than these he will do; because I am going to the Father"* (John 14:12).

Brenna McCormick shares that the gift of miracles initiates, restores, and strengthens faith in God.[2]

131

Initiates Faith

In Acts 9, God asked a disciple named Ananias to go to Saul and restore his sight. Knowing that Saul had been sent to the area to arrest anyone who followed Jesus, Ananias followed God's commands. Immediately upon placing his hands on Saul, Saul's sight returned, he was baptized, and he began to preach in the name of Jesus.

Ananias chose to listen to God and do what He said, and Ananias' faith was strengthened as God empowered him to perform a miracle. And, because of his faithfulness, Saul began to follow Jesus in a way that "astonished" and "baffled" those who knew the person he was before he met Jesus (Acts 9:21-22).

Restores Faith

In Acts 9, a disciple named Tabitha became sick and died. Her loved ones called for Peter to come and pray for her. God empowered him to bring Tabitha back to life, and because of this miracle, "many people believed in the Lord" (Acts 9:42).

God used Peter to perform a miracle that led to the restoration of physical life for Tabitha and spiritual life for many others.

Strengthens Faith

In Acts 16, Paul and Silas were arrested after casting a demon out of a slave girl. Despite being stripped, beaten, and thrown in jail, the men "were praying and singing hymns to God, and the other prisoners were listening to them" (Acts 16:25).

The miracle was a catalyst for an opportunity for Paul and Silas to strengthen their faith in God through prayer, praise, and petition, and their attitudes allowed the other prisoners to see the strength that accompanies faith in Jesus truly.

Yes, there are some who will be and are endowed with the same gift of miracles that Jesus Himself demonstrated while walking on earth. Yes, there are some who will be and are blessed with the same gift of miracles that Jesus Himself demonstrated while walking on earth.

On January 19, 2015, John Smith, fourteen, drowned when he fell through the ice while standing on Lake Sainte Louise in Missouri. Doctors worked for 45 minutes, trying to revive him. Despite their heroic efforts, they concluded John wouldn't survive.[3]

That's when Joyce, John's mom, went into the emergency room where her son lay dead on the table. Instead of saying goodbye, she speaks life. She goes over to his feet, puts her hands on his feet, and says, 'Holy Spirit, bring back my son.' Next thing you know, John came back to life." Doctors were still convinced that John wouldn't recover, considering how long he had gone without oxygen. But, to their shock, he not only recovered, but today it's as if he never went through the deadly ordeal. The doctors said, "It's nothing but God."

The Gifts of the Spirit Summarized and Assessed

From the list provided in Scripture, which gifts has God given to you? Sometimes the very gifts which are strongest are those for which we do not even see in ourselves. Often, the possession of an

133

innate strength in a gift will cause us to doubt its significance. Two ways in which to approach this evaluation are:

1. Quietly go into a place of solitude and in prayer and meditation, ask the Lord to search your heart, to reveal to you the gifts that He has bestowed upon you, so that you may begin using them to their fullest extent as purposed by God.

2. Gather with other brothers and sisters and discuss this list with them. Help each other identify what gifts you all may possess and how to use them to honor the Lord daily.

It may be interesting to compare your self-evaluation with those in your group or even with your family. In Hebrews 10:24 (NIV) it states, *"And let us consider how we may spur one another on toward love and good deeds..."* Furthermore, in the following verse it says, *"...not giving up meeting together, as some are in the habit of doing, but encouraging one another---and all the more as you see the Day approaching."*

This is a perfect example from scripture of fellow Christians, thinking of, as Hebrews 10:24 puts it, ways to *"spur one another on toward love and good deeds."*

REFLECTION

Review (What struck you personally?)

Revelation (What is God saying to you?)

Response (What are you going to do today)

Chapter 7

Empowerment of the GIFT

"But you will receive power when the Holy Spirit has come upon you; and you shall be My witnesses both in Jerusalem, and in all Judea, and Samaria, and as far as the remotest parts of the earth."

(Acts 1:8)

God has given you His Holy Spirit, He has endowed you with unique specific gifts, and if that is not enough, He has supercharged you with His power to carry out the purpose of your gifts!

Steven J. Lawson[1], in his book, The Kind of Preaching God Blesses, shares how 19th-century evangelist Dwight L. Moody was a man mightily used by God even though he was not formally educated or well-versed with the English language's proper use. What was the secret to his success? At one point, Moody was to have a campaign in England. An elderly pastor protested, "Why do we need this 'Mr. Moody'? He was uneducated, inexperienced, and he went on and on about how unqualified Moody was. Who does he think he is anyway? Does he think he has a monopoly on the Holy Spirit?" A younger, wiser pastor rose and responded, "No, but the Holy Spirit has a monopoly on Mr. Moody"

When God takes hold of your life through the indwelling and infilling of the Holy Spirit, you will not have to rely on anything external, for He will do in you and for you what you can never do for yourself. The supernatural power of the Holy Spirit takes over, and you then become fully energized to carry out the purpose of the gifts which has been implanted in you by God!

Listen, dear friends, the reason why your life is a gift is that you have been given the greatest gift of all in the form of the Holy Spirit. In the book of Acts 1:1-5 (NIV), we read this, *"In my former book, Theophilus, I wrote about all that Jesus began to do and to teach until the day he was taken up to heaven, after giving instructions through the Holy Spirit to the apostles he had chosen. After his suffering, he presented himself to them and gave many convincing proofs that he was alive. He appeared to them over a period of forty days and spoke about the kingdom of God."*

"On one occasion, while he was eating with them, he gave them this command; 'Do not leave Jerusalem, but wait for the gift my Father promised, which you have heard me speak about. For John baptized with water, but in a few days, you will be baptized with the Holy Spirit.'"

Sure enough, just as Jesus promises, that glorious day of Pentecost came just as revealed in Acts 2: 1-4 (NIV) when *"...all the believers were meeting together in one place. Suddenly a sound like the blowing of a violent wind came from heaven and filled the whole house where they were sitting. They saw what seemed to be tongues of fire that separated and came to rest on each of them. All of them were filled with the Holy Spirit and began to speak in tongues as the Spirit enabled them."*

At that moment, Peter stepped forward with the eleven other apostles, and one of the gifts of the Spirit, that of prophecy was activated in an extraordinary way! Filled with the Holy Spirit, he stepped in with great confidence and power of the Spirit and began to prophesy! The result of his preaching was this, *"So then, those who had received his word were baptized; and that day there were added three thousand souls"* (Acts 2:41).

The Apostle Peter was a formerly uneducated man with little to no human power and influence. Yet, he was suddenly endowed with the power of God and began to speak, consequently winning over thousands of people to the Lord!

Was this because Peter was a natural orator, a highly educated charismatic figure in that of himself? No, of course not; it was because what he received came from God and was activated through the power of the Holy Spirit to accomplish God's divine purpose. And God has given each one of us gifts and the Holy Spirit to activate these gifts in a powerful and supernatural way!

The Holy Spirit is the very presence of God within you, that is ever willing and ready to activate the incredible gifts that He has entrusted with you. How then is the switch turned on so that your gift and the power of God are activated from within to its fullest, just as it was with Peter and the other apostles?

The operative phrase in answer to this all-important question is to "be filled with the Spirit." In Ephesians 5:18, we see this powerful phrase and teaching reappear, whereby the Apostle Paul exhorts his readers to *"... be filled with the Spirit."*

It is one thing to have the Holy Spirit, which every believer receives and possesses from the day that they believed and accepted Jesus Christ as his Savior, and it is another thing *to be filled with the Spirit.* To be saved means to have the Holy Spirit abide in you, and to be filled with the Holy Spirit means to have the power of God released from within you, to do in you what only God can do.

In essence, it is the full living expression and experience of what the apostle meant when in Galatians 2:20 he states, *"I have been crucified with Christ; and it is no longer I who live, but Christ lives in me ...",* and further in Philippians 1:21 declares, *"For to me to live is Christ..."*

As we go back to Ephesians 5:18, we see the direct instructions from the Lord that say, *"And do not get drunk with wine, in which there is debauchery, but be filled with the Spirit."*

Isn't it interesting that the Bible makes such a contrast, the contrast of drunkenness with such a holy experience as being filled with the Spirit? The difference could not be sharper. The element that makes it common is the two experiences of being drunk and filled with the Holy Spirit. Both experiences take over the faculties of a human being in terms of his thinking, judgments, desires, language, and behavior. The consequences and rewards of both submissions are in sharp contrast to one another. One results in a being that is out of control and quite frequently can put himself and others in danger, and the other is beautiful, divine, and full of control that brings tremendous blessings to both himself and others that are present.

Perhaps we have been in a situation where we have witnessed a person that had become increasingly drunk. What happens? The more that person drinks, the more that person begins to lose control of his reasoning, speech, and behavior, to the point where frequently a person who is intoxicated no longer thinks and acts as one should. As scripture states, this leads to evil and all kinds of unwise, uncontrolled, and excessive behaviors that can carry dire consequences. Perhaps we have heard the term when a person is in a drunken state, "That's not Bob speaking, that's the alcohol speaking." Or maybe someone was trying to explain away their unsavory behavior by saying, "I was drunk," as if that was an acceptable excuse.

To put it into perspective, a tragic amount people die in this world from alcohol-related incidences. The evidence of alcohol consumption on the entire body, especially the brain, heart, pancreas, mouth, liver, and immune system, is well documented. The annals of history are filled with disparaging stories of lost relationships, lost employment and careers, lives and families destroyed by what today is called alcoholism. The courtrooms are filled with cases relating to physical assaults, domestic violence, and all sorts of reckless indiscretions caused by excessive drinking.

The Apostle says in Ephesians 5, *"be not drunk."* In some way, he is saying, "do not do as those who do not know Christ do; you have something far better, purer, holier, and empowering than alcohol, the Holy Spirit within." So now, instead of consuming alcohol, consume from the presence of the Holy Spirit with you, drink from His fountain, and be filled with the Spirit. Drink and submit to the Spirit continually, and as you do, the Holy Spirit will fill your life, whereby it will no longer be you living, but Christ living in you. People will be startled because you will have taken on the very persona of Jesus Christ.

What is this? Why it is the Fruit of the Spirit as mentioned in Galatians 5:22-23. This will show and become overwhelmingly evident in the expression of your thoughts, words, and actions. What will show up is *"love, joy, peace, patience, kindness, goodness, faithfulness, gentleness, and self-control."*

As you let go and let God, you will become a conduit for all these divine virtues. Your life will begin to express strange and unusual human behaviors such as

- Loving your enemies.
- Experiencing an inner joy that is *unspeakable and full of glory, a peace that surpasses understanding.*
- A kindness towards all.
- A divine patience.
- An expression of goodness in the midst of evil.
- A faithfulness to God and others.
- Gentleness in your speech.
- A demeanor of godly self-control.
- A supernatural ability not to react, but rather respond with grace, wisdom, and love, just as Jesus did.

People will not necessarily see you, but instead, they will see Jesus in you. I honestly believe that the greatest compliment a believer can receive is when people see and say, "I see Jesus in you."

Remember the analogy we alluded to earlier about a person intoxicated by alcohol when people would say, 'Oh, that isn't 'Bob' speaking, that's the alcohol speaking."

When you are filled with the Spirit of God, people can't help but notice that there is a divine power that is in control of your life that supersedes any natural human behavior. You are or will be empowered with the Holy Spirit!

The wisdom, love, joy, and thankfulness that pours out of Spirit Life dumfounds the world because it is supernatural! It is through this empowerment that we can turn the other cheek when someone strikes us, to bless those that curse us, to love those that hate us, to give thanks to God under every circumstance, to rejoice in Him always, and experience the tremendous unleashing of the spiritual gifts in you. This is what it means to be the salt and light in this world!

Jesus says in John 15:5, *"for apart from Me you can do nothing."* This is so true! The living Spirit cannot be experienced unless you are in the Spirit! It is not your works, but Christ manifested in you that is at work.

As much as one tries, and in as much as one, in theory, would like to, by human effort, one cannot fulfill the commandments of God; only Christ can! It takes that supernatural experience of the infilling of the Holy Spirit to do these things! It is impossible without Christ at work in you, but all things are possible through His power. It is what Jesus meant when in Matthew 19:26, *"And looking at them, Jesus said to them, 'With people this is impossible, but with God all things are possible.'"*

If there is one thing to understand about the Christian life, no one has the power to live it, except for Christ. Only He can truly live the Christian life, and so if we are to live the life to which we are called, we need to completely get out of the way, surrender to the Spirit of Christ within us and let Him live His life through us. That is what the Spirit-filled life is! None of me and all of Him expressed through my mind and body.

Let us take for a moment the analogy of an empty glove. A glove in and of itself cannot do anything; it is just a glove. It has no power to pick things or hold on to something. The glove alone is powerless, but when you put your hand in the glove, then and only then can the glove function with power and purpose. So, it is with us. Like that glove, we are powerless and useless without God, but God through His Spirit fills our lives, just like that glove becomes empowered to do things that otherwise would not be possible without the hand of God at work in your life.

Being filled with the Holy Spirit, in essence, means to be filled with God, to be empowered to live the victorious Christian life!

Sin's Obstruction:

Now the question comes, if we were designed to live in such a manner, why does it seem that so many professing Christians fall short of experiencing this power in their lives? They claim to love the Lord, but their lives fall short of expressing this divine and victorious power, called the infilling of the Spirit.

The answer is short and simple – conscious sin. Willful sin is what obstructs a believer from fully experiencing the power of God. It does so because sin goes right against the core of what is needed to be filled with the Spirit, which is a complete, unconditional surrender of our lives to God. One can be saved yet still be held in the bondage of sin that renders one powerless. As long as a believer still desires to hold on and control various aspects of his life, he will not experience the infilling of the Spirit.

Instead of turning it over entirely to God if we want to run our lives, He will not force the matter. If we feel we could do a better job than God in driving the vehicle of our lives, then to our detriment, God will not interfere. It is like the famous song recorded by Carrie Underwood[2], "Jesus Take the Wheel." So often, we insist on doing things our way, be it for lack of faith, pride, stubbornness, or selfishness, until we get a wake-up call that finally reaches us. The refrain of the song, written by Brett James, Hillary Lindsey, and Gordie Sampson, goes something like this,

"Jesus, take the wheel
Take it from my hands
Cause I can't do this on my own
I'm letting go
So give me one more chance

And save me from this road I'm on

Jesus, take the wheel.

Oh, take it, take it from me."

What a simple but powerful song that represents a metaphor for our lives! We could do the driving, or we could let God do the driving. The choice is ours, however, and it is quite a difficult one to make for most.

Until we finally come to the point in our lives where we finally recognize and say, "God, that's it, I can't do this anymore. I don't have the strength and ability to run my own life." That, ironically, is the beginning whereby God can continue His work in you!

If you think you may be the only believer who struggles with sin, be it pride, anger, resentment, self-righteousness, hypocrisy, fear, or lack of willingness and faith, you can take comfort in knowing that this is all part of the battle and familiar to every believer.

Even the Apostle Paul, of whom God used to write most of the New Testament, knew this struggle. The Apostle Paul writes of this struggle in Romans 7:15-20 (NIV):

"I do not understand what I do. For what I want to do I do not do, but what I hate I do. And if I do what I do not want to do, I agree that the law is good. As it is, it is no longer I myself who do it, but it is sin living in me. For I know that good itself does not dwell in me, that is, in my sinful nature.[a] For I have the desire to do what is good, but I cannot carry it out. For I do not do the good

I want to do, but the evil I do not want to do—this I keep on doing. Now if I do what I do not want to do, it is no longer I who do it, but it is sin living in me that does it."

What a dilemma! Yet it is a struggle that all believers face, a willingness, and desire to do what is good, right, and honorable to God, but sinfulness attempts to obstruct us every step of the way.

With the problem of sin, Dwight L. Moody put it this way, "I have had more trouble with myself than with any other man."[3] Although we are believers, our sinful nature still wars with our new nature constantly.

Our struggle could be likened to the story of a Native-American Christian who went to a missionary for counsel. He was very much troubled by the spiritual conflict going on within his heart. He wanted to do what God wanted for him, but he was frequently disobeying God. He found that he was prone to do evil things, even as he did before he became a Christian. The man described this conflict within himself as a dogfight. He said to the missionary,

"It is as though I have a black dog and a white dog inside me fighting each other constantly." The black dog, he explained, represented evil, and the white dog represented good.

The missionary asked him, "Which dog wins the fight within you?"

After several moments of silence, the native said, "The dog that wins is the one I feed, and the dog that loses is the one I starve."[4]

147

This illustrates what each believer must contend with, a constant inner battle between two powerful forces: our old sinful nature and our new nature. The process in theological terms is "sanctification."

People who do not know Christ do not have that struggle, for the Holy Spirit does not abide in them. At times they may struggle between a good or bad conscious, but not a constant, internal warfare. That experience is unique to the Christian.

It is not uncommon that a believer who possesses Christ in their lives and does not live according to the power of the Spirit within can find himself even more miserable than an unbeliever. It is a terrible predicament to find oneself in.

In this state of sin, the believer is hindered from trusting in the supernatural power of God, the infilling of the Holy Spirit. David the psalmist knew this, for he stated, *"If I regard wickedness in my heart, the Lord would not hear"* (Psalm 66:18).

To live in a stubborn and willful state of sin while, at the same time, asking God for His help and guidance does not work. It is a direct contradiction to itself. It is like trying to drive with the emergency brakes on. Your life cannot be set free in victory unless you let go of the brakes called sin.

Sin will always be present in our lives, like a wolf at the door waiting to make its entrance and keep us from experiencing the fullness of God in our lives. 1 John 1:8 states, *"If we say we have no sin, we deceive ourselves, and the truth is not in us."* Yet in the following verse, it gives us the wonderful remedy and escape from our sin. For it states, *"If we confess our sins, He is faithful and righteous, so that He will forgive us our sins, and to cleanse us from all unrighteousness"* (1 John 1:9).

In Proverbs 28:13, we see the difference between the consequences of holding on to sin versus the blessing of confessing and renouncing our sins. *"One who conceals his wrongdoings will not prosper, But whoever confesses and abandons them will find compassion."*

Acknowledgment and confessing our sins is the first step towards restoring our fellowship with God and putting ourselves in a place before Him where He can continue His mighty work in us.

Sin has a draining consequence on our lives and thus makes us ineffective for God. Yet when we acknowledge our sins and confess before our Lord, he restores our joy and our strength.

This reality is reflected in Psalm 32:3-5 (NIV), *"When I kept silent, my bones wasted away through my groaning all day long. For day and night your hand was heavy on me; my strength was sapped as in the heat of summer. Then I acknowledged my sin to you and did not cover up my iniquity. I said, 'I will confess my transgressions to the LORD.' And you forgave the guilt of my sin."*

In Acts 3:19, it states, *"Therefore repent and return, so that your sins may be wiped away, in order that times of refreshing may come from the presence of the Lord."* The retention of our sin weighs heavy, but the act of confessing and repenting our sins refreshes us and sets us free!

In Hebrews 12:1 (NIV) we are exhorted to, *"...throw off everything that hinders and the sin that so easily entangles. And let us run with perseverance the race marked out for us..."*

As believers, before we can experience being *filled with the Spirit,* we must first acknowledge and turn away from our sins.

At this point, how does one become filled with the Spirit? Can any and every believer who confesses and repents of their sins experience the infilling of the Holy Spirit? The answer to the question from Scripture is a resounding, "Yes!"

Being Filled with the Spirit.

Firstly, we are instructed and commanded to be filled, and ultimately, His will, that we are filled with the Spirit. God never asks us to do something which we are unable to do or experience under His power! Therefore, know that the infilling of the Spirit is not designed or reserved for a special few in the body of Christ, but rather it is God's will that we all be filled with His Spirit!

Let us go back for a moment to Ephesians 5, whereby we see this specific instruction. Starting with verse 17, *"Therefore do not be foolish, but understand what the will of Lord is."* This verse is especially important to note, because here the Word exhorts something specific pertaining to the reality of God's will. Ephesians 5:18 (NIV) says, *"Do not get drunk on wine, which leads to debauchery. Instead, be filled with the Spirit..."*

It is God's will that you be filled with the Spirit!

Let us look at what the rest of Scripture which states how God responds to anyone who prays according to His will. 1 John 5:14-

150

15 says, *"This is the confidence which we have toward Him, that, if we ask anything according to His will, He hears us. And if we know that He hears us, whatever we ask, we know that we have the requests which we have asked from Him."*

In the same way that we have come to salvation through faith in Jesus Christ, we also come to the experience of the infilling of the Holy Spirit. It is through asking in prayer and through faith that one becomes filled with the Spirit!

When we are filled with the Spirit, then we will begin to know and experience *what it means to walk in Spirit* (Galatians 5:16), *to live in the Spirit* (Galatians 5:25) and *to pray in the Spirit* (Ephesians 6:18), and *to speak in the Spirit* (Matthew 10:20). In fact, you will be doing everything in the Spirit and to the glory of God. It will no longer be you living on your own, as the Apostle Paul put in Galatians 2:20, *"but Christ lives in me."* You will be walking, living, and speaking in the power of God! What will be clear and evident is the revelation of the very fruit of the Spirit, spoken about in Galatians 5:22-23.

You will begin to do beautiful things under the Spirit's power, such as loving your enemies, turning the other cheek, going the extra mile, speaking with power, wisdom, and confidence, and in some cases where the gift has been given to you to do so, speaking in tongues, interpreting tongues, healing the sick and even casting out demons.

One definitive result of the infilling of the Spirit is supercharging and supernaturally activating the gifts that the Holy Spirit has given to fulfill His purpose.

As a final note, it is essential to know that the infilling of the Spirit is not a one-time experience, but a moment-by-moment experience that occurs as we surrender our lives completely to Him. In Ephesians 5:18 whereby we are instructed to *"be filled with the Spirit."* The original Greek word or term for "be" is in this case translated to "being," and in others, being filled with the Spirit continually! In doing so, you will experience the very power of God in your conduct, in your speech, and in your life.

Being filled with the Spirit is not something that can be accomplished through intellectual means, but rather is something only prayer can achieve. If you are a believer in Jesus Christ, and have been holding onto certain areas of your life which prevent you from experiencing this, isn't it time to go to God in prayer, acknowledge and confess your sins to Him, ask the Lord to give you a repentant heart and in doing so to fill every part of your being with His Holy Spirit?

If this is something for which God is speaking to your heart right now, I would encourage you to go to God in prayer about right now, and He will fill you with His Holy Spirit. You may or may not feel something because of this, for we walk by faith and not by feeling. However, one thing is sure, God will not hold back, not for a moment; the experience of being filled with His Holy Spirit is immediately available if you ask it of Him

REFLECTION

Review (What struck you personally?)

Revelation (What is God saying to you?)

Response (What are you going to do today)

Chapter 8

Reward of the GIFT

"His Lord said to him, 'Well done, good and faithful servant! You have been faithful over a few things, I will set you over many things. Enter into the joy of your lord.'"

(Matthew 25:21)

As my friend James L. Capra, former International Director of Operations for the Drug Enforcement Agency, would repeat time and time, "This life is so temporal, I just want to finish well." What a wonderful reminder, and he is right! This life as we know it here on earth, with our earthy bodies, is just temporal and is but a flash in the light of eternity!

Life goes by amazingly fast! For example, statistics indicate that the average life expectancy for women living in the United States is approximately 81 years, while the life expectancy for men is about 76 years.

British missionary C.T. Studd[1] wrote a beautiful poem, "Only One Life," that puts our time here on earth into its proper perspective

"Two little lines I heard one day, Traveling along life's busy way; Bringing conviction to my heart, And from my mind would not depart;

Only one life, 'twill soon be past, Only what's done for Christ will last.

155

Only one life, yes only one, Soon will its fleeting hours be done;
Then, in 'that day' my Lord to meet, And stand before His
Judgment seat;
Only one life,' twill soon be past, Only what's done for Christ will
last.

Only one life, the still small voice, Gently pleads for a better
choice
Bidding me selfish aims to leave, And to God's holy will to cleave;
Only one life, 'twill soon be past, Only what's done for Christ will
last.

Only one life, a few brief years, Each with its burdens, hopes, and
fears;
Each with its days I must fulfill, living for self or in His will;
Only one life, 'twill soon be past, Only what's done for Christ will
last.

When this bright world would tempt me sore, When Satan would a
victory score;
When self would seek to have its way, Then help me Lord with joy
to say;
Only one life, 'twill soon be past, Only what's done for Christ will
last.

Give me Father, a purpose deep, In joy or sorrow Thy word to
keep;
Faithful and true what e'er the strife, Pleasing Thee in my daily
life;

Only one life, 'twill soon be past, Only what's done for Christ will last.

Oh let my love with fervor burn, And from the world now let me turn;

Living for Thee, and Thee alone, Bringing Thee pleasure on Thy throne;

Only one life, "twill soon be past, Only what's done for Christ will last.

Only one life, yes only one, Now let me say, "Thy will be done";

And when at last I'll hear the call, I know I'll say 'twas worth it all";

Only one life,' twill soon be past, Only what's done for Christ will last."

The years go by quickly before we know it, and that is if we survive without some unexpected incident that takes us home before then, we will soon find ourselves at the end of life's journey here on earth.

For some of us, it takes a lifetime to realize how fragile and fleeting it is until the reality of the brevity of life suddenly hits us. The sooner one realizes this, the more years he will have left to really discover and experience the true essence of life and his calling here on earth.

Scripture states, *"So then, be careful how you walk, not an unwise people, but as wise, making the most of your time, because the days are evil"* (Ephesians 5:15-16).

It has been said that "your life is a gift from God, and how you live is your gift to God." The ultimate purpose of our lives is to glorify God, and we glorify God by fulfilling His will and keeping His commandments. The greatest of the commandments that completes and fulfills the entire book of the law is this, *"Love the Lord your God with all your heart and with all your soul and with all your mind. This is the first and greatest commandment. And the second is like it: 'Love your neighbor as yourself'"* (Matthew 22:37-39, NIV).

Supreme love for God and others is at the center of what it means to be a GIFT, both to God and others!

We are only here on earth as we know it for a short time. The life and the gifts we were given are not from ourselves, lest we should boast in them, but God gives them to love and serve Him and others. And in doing so, He activates the power of the GIFT in you to love and serve others.

We are not called to be successful, although if we remain in Him, we will be. But, more importantly, we are called to be faithful! If faithfulness to God is embedded in our hearts, God will take care of the rest.

The daily cry of our hearts should be this, "Faithfulness Lord to You is what I long for, faithfulness to You Oh Lord is what I need!"

Soon, that day will come when we meet our Lord face-to-face and will hear the blessed words, *"Well done, good and faithful servant!"* O, how unspeakably beautiful those words will be, as He places the crown of righteousness upon your head.

In 2 Timothy 4:8 we read, *"in the future there is reserved for me the crown of righteousness, which the Lord, the righteous Judge, will award to me on that day; and not only to me, but also to all who have loved His appearing."*

This crown of righteousness is *"to obtain an inheritance which is imperishable, undefiled, and will not fade away, reserved in heaven for you"* (1 Peter 1:4). Furthermore, the Bible tells us that there is a wonderous hope that awaits us, as it is written, *"Things which eye has not seen and ear has not heard, And which have not entered the human heart, All that God has prepared for those who love Him"* (1 Corinthians 2:9).

Oh, how life on earth is fleeting and brief, but how eternity with God is unimaginably rewarding and blessed. Though we are here on earth for a short time, we await a reward in Heaven that is eternal!

In Proverbs, we read, *"When a wicked person dies, his expectation will perish, And the hope of strong people perishes"* (Proverbs 11:7), *"... but the righteous has a refuge when he dies"* (Proverbs 14:32).

And "What a Day That Will Be!" The hymnal writer, Jim Hill wrote the lyrics:
"There is coming a day
When no heartache shall come
No more clouds in the sky

No more tears to dim the eye

All is peace forever more

On that happy golden shore

What a day, glorious day that will be.

What a day that will be

When my Jesus I shall see

And I look upon His face

The One who saved me by His grace

When He takes me by the hand

And leads me through the Promised Land

What a day, glorious day that will be

There'll be no sorrow there

No more burdens to bear

No more sickness, no pain

No more parting over there

And forever I will be

With the One who died for me

What a day, glorious day that will be."

There is no question that as we toil here on earth, we will face many trials, heartaches, and temptations. There will be times of suffering, as there is with all. *"Indeed, and all who want to live a godly life in a godly way in Christ Jesus will be persecuted"* (2 Timothy 3:12). However, the difference between you and those who do not know Christ is that you have an enduring hope, strength, joy, and peace that transcends any hardship you can ever face here on earth.

160

The apostle Paul wrote this, *"I want to know Christ—yes, to know the power of his resurrection and participation in his sufferings, becoming like him in his death, and so, somehow, attaining to the resurrection from the dead.*

Not that I have already obtained all this, or have already arrived at my goal, but I press on to take hold of that for which Christ Jesus took hold of me. Brothers and sisters, I do not consider myself yet to have taken hold of it. But one thing I do: Forgetting what is behind and straining toward what is ahead, I press on toward the goal to win the prize for which God has called me heavenward in Christ Jesus" (Philippians 3:10-14, NIV).

Furthermore, in 2 Timothy 1:12 Paul states, *"... for I know whom I have believed, and I am convinced that He is able to protect that what I have entrusted to Him until that day."*

What day is that? That glorious day when we will meet the Lord Jesus our Savior, face-to-face.

Be encouraged brothers and sisters, for the Bible assures you that the good work that God has begun in you will be completed until that day. Philippians 1:6 states, *"For I am confident of this very thing, that He who began a good work among you will complete it by the day of Christ Jesus."*

In closing, there will be three types of people reading this book regarding where you find yourself on the timeline of life. It may be towards,

1. The End of Your Life

2. The Middle of Your Life

3. The Beginning of Your Life

No one except God knows when one's life can suddenly come to an end. Who knew that Natalie, my precious daughter's life would be taken at such a young age?

1. The End of Your Life:

As you are growing older and seeing and experiencing your mortality, the things you were once able to do seem harder, and your eyesight, hearing, or physical strength, in general, are not what they once were. A sobering realization begins to set in, revealing that your days are numbered, and you will soon be leaving this earth. Perhaps this realization begins to intensify for many around their mid-fifties. As indicated earlier, if you are the average American, this means you have approximately, statistically speaking, only about 20 years left before you make the great transition.

Perhaps as you read this, you find yourself at the very end of your life here on earth. There is hardly anyone closer to the realization of his death than the criminal on the cross hanging beside Jesus, as described in Luke 23:39-43 (NIV).

As one criminal on the other side of Jesus hurled insults at Him, the other cried criminal rebuked him, saying, *"'Don't you fear God,'" he said, 'since you are under the same sentence? We are punished justly, for we are getting what our deeds deserve. But this man has done nothing wrong.' Then he said, 'Jesus, remember me when you come into your kingdom.'"*

What was Jesus's response?

"Jesus answered him, 'Truly I tell you, today you will be with me in paradise.'"

Even in an extreme case such as this, in a person's dying moments, the gift of God is readily available to whomsoever repents and believes. So long as a person has breath in him, there is hope, all the way to one's dying day.

At this point, one may wonder, "Well, that is extremely touching, but what does that have to do with fulfilling one's gifts?" The criminal on the cross had squandered his life and was to die a criminal's death. How could his life be a gift?

Upon reflection, I wondered about that too, asking the same question to myself, but then came the fantastic realization of the wonder, mercy, and wisdom of God's grace. The story of this criminal is a perfect representation of the redemption story that is possible for any of us through Christ's sacrifice on the cross.

Firstly came the reminder that no matter what we do for God, it cannot ever buy our redemption in terms of service. That it is by grace through faith that we are saved, and the good that we do, is not us but Christ in us as written in Ephesians 2:8-9, *"For by grace you have been saved, through faith; and that is not of yourselves, it is the gift of God; not a result of works, so that no one can boast."*

The second realization is this, and it pertains directly to the question, what did this criminal ever do to use his gifts for Jesus? The answer is absolutely nothing! There is nothing any of us can do but to receive from Him. The criminal's conversation with Christ as he died on the cross has been retold millions of times throughout the centuries. It serves as a powerful testimony to the marvelous grace of God. Even in his dying moments, not only did God forgive him and promise him eternal life, but the account of his life continues to serve to this day as a powerful testimony to the message of the amazing grace of God! This man's account continues to serve as a powerful message and gift of understanding, hope, and salvation to others. He may be physically gone, but his message of repentance and hope lives on to this day.

The core message is, we do not have to wait until our dying day to turn to God and have Him give us a beautiful and purposeful gift. We can do it now, today!

One of the most outrageous lies that the devil will ever tell anyone is that "it is too late, you have blown your chance, you wasted and squandered your life and are beyond hope and redemption." That is a lie straight from the pit of hell!

In the Book of Joel 2 (NIV), we read *"'Even now,' declares the LORD, 'return to me with all your heart, with fasting and weeping and mourning.' Rend your heart and not your garments. Return to the LORD your God, for he is gracious and compassionate, slow to anger and abounding in love."*

The Lord then promises, *"I will repay you for the years the locusts have eaten—the great locust and the young locust, the other locusts and the locust swarm—my great army that I sent among you. You will have plenty to eat, until you are full, and you will praise the name of the LORD your God, who has worked wonders for you..."* (Joel 2:12-13, 25-26).

He will repay you for the years the locusts have eaten! This is our God; He never lets anything go to waste if we turn to Him.

If you have not done so already, or you find yourself at a point in your life reflecting on the apparent years lost, take hope, turn now to the Lord and He will restore your soul and re-ignite the gifts that are from within. It is never too late to turn back to the Lord!

2. The Middle of Your Life

Let's define the middle of your life as ages 30-55. These are often considered the prime years of your life when all the engines are wide open! This is the period when you have learned enough about life to find direction and stability, and you may find yourself at your best in terms of the combination of your strength and insight.

These are the years of great opportunity, the years whereby you can use your gifts and skills for the sake of the kingdom of God and for foolish and selfish endeavors more than any other time in your life.

Regrettably, during this period of my life, I only focused on what I got from others. My identity was in the world. I believed the

165

more possessions I owned, the better the positions I held and what people thought of me was what determined my self-worth. As you might imagine, I was miserable. I struggled, remained frustrated and had limited opportunities for success. While my professional career seemed to be on track, my personal life was full of slips, trips and falls, predominantly from ages 30-45.

3. The Beginning of Your Life

If you find yourself at the beginning stage of your life, around 25 or younger, you are at the most exciting and pivotal point in your life. Listen, kid! You have your whole life ahead of you! It is exciting!

The decisions you make at this stage of your life, the earlier, the better, will determine the quality and course of your life from this point onward. You need not make the mistakes like I did before you learn, but rather, learn from those that have gone before you.

I have been asked, what is the best advice you can give a young person who is just starting off in life? First and foremost, stay away from temptations, Proverbs 5:8 (NIV). *"Temptations occur because of our emotional state of needing something only God can offer. Satan manipulated me through my emotions. As you just read, I was tempted by what the world could give me in order to feel successful and failed miserably until my identity was rooted in Christ. Therefore, make no provision for your temptations of the flesh. Get rid of all distractions and focus on going about God's work."*

Secondly, Proverbs 1:5 encourages us to never stop learning, *"A wise person will hear and increase in learning, And a person understanding will acquire wise counsel."* People who believe they are better than others quickly reject the advice from people willing to help them. They let their ego get in the way of self-improvement.

Thirdly, stay humble. Once you are blessed with wisdom, don't consider yourself better than others. The Bible is evident that God resists the proud but blesses a humble heart.

Remember, pride comes before a fall. When you find yourself looking down on others or bragging about your accomplishments, remember that God is the one who provides your blessings. I was fortunate enough to be given numerous accolades while serving 21 years in the Air Force. I can honestly say, without the help and support of others, none of the awards would have been possible.

In a beautiful poem called Season of Man, Steve and Annie Chapman[3] summarize our lives on earth with the following words.

"I am the springtime, when everything seems so fine.

Whether rain or sunshine, you will find me playing.

Days full of pretending.

When a dime is a lot to be spending.

A time when life is beginning.

I am the springtime.

I am the summer. When the days are warm and longer.

When the call comes to wander, but I can't go far from home.

When the girls become a mystery.

167

When you're barely passing history.

And thinking old is when you're thirty.

I am the summer.

And I am the autumn days. When changes come so many ways.

Looking back I stand amazed that time has gone so quickly.

When love is more than feelings.

It's fixing bikes and painting ceilings.

It's when you feel a cold wind coming.

I am the autumn days.

I am the winter. When days are cold and bitter.

And the days I can remember number more than the days to come.

When you ride, instead of walking.

When you barely hear the talking.

And goodbyes are said too often.

I am the winter...

But I'll see springtime in heaven,

and it will last forever."

Where do you find yourself today in the season of your life? Are you experiencing the Spring, Summer, Autumn, or Winter?

May I encourage you at this time to reflect deeply on your life, on what is really important? Learn from the lives of others who have gone before you, derive the insights of the meaning and fragility of our mortal existence and to ponder from this point onward your response to the Gift of Life that God has given you through Jesus Christ His Son.

Therefore, when the final day of winter in your life arrives, when you lay down all the labors, trophies, and accomplishments and you make the transition to eternity and face God, you will be greeted with blessed words of our Lord,

"Well done my good and faithful servant!"

REFLECTION

Review (What struck you personally?)

Revelation (What is God saying to you?)

Response (What are you going to do today)

Notes

Chapter 1. You Are A GIFT

1. "John Newton." Wikiquote, https://en.wikiquote.org/wiki/John_Newton.

2. *The Spurgeon Study Bible.* (2017). Holman Bible Publishers.

3. Archon Sofo. The Unbounded Spirit, https://theunboundedspirit.com/heaven-and-hell-the-parable-of-the-long- spoons/.

4. *Prayer of Saint Francis of Assisi.* Wikipedia, https://en.wikipedia.org/wiki/Prayer_of_Saint_Francis.

Chapter 2. Author of the GIFT

1. "He Owns the Cattle (On a Thousand Hills)", © 1948 John W. Peterson Music Company. All rights reserved. Used by permission.

Chapter 3. Beware of the GIFT Robber

1. Sun Tzu. Brainy Quote, https://www.brainyquote.com/quotes/sun_tzu_155752.

2. D. L. Moody. Sermon Quotes, https://sermonquotes.com/trouble/14346-i-have-more-trouble-with-d-l-moody-than-with-any-other-man-ive-ever-met-dwight-l-moody.html.

3. John Newton. Timeless Truths, https://library.timelesstruths.org/music/Amazing_Grace/.

4. Helen Howarth Lemmel. hymnal.net, https://www.hymnal.net/en/hymn/h/645.

5. Eugene Bartlett. PopularHyms.com, https://popularhymns.com/victory-in-jesus.

Chapter 4. Defenders of the GIFT

1. Stu Weber. (2001). *Spirit warriors.* Multnomah Publishers.

2. Lee Colan. Inc. Magazine, https://www.inc.com/lee-colan/whos-packing-your-parachute_1.html.

Chapter 5. Purpose of the GIFT

1. John Donne. Bartleby.com, https://www.bartleby.com/73/134.html.

Chapter 6. Manifestation of the GIFT

1. R.G. Letourneau. Wikipedia,
   https://en.wikipedia.org/wiki/R._G._LeTourneau.
2. Brenna McCormick. New Spring Church, https://newspring.cc/articles/how-to-know-the-gift-of-miracles-when-you-see-it.
3. Caleb Parke. Fox News, https://www.foxnews.com/faith-values/god-still-does-the-impossible-the-incredible-true-story-behind-the-faith-based-film-breakthrough

Chapter 7. Empowerment of the GIFT

1. Steven J. Lawson. (2013). *The kind of preaching god blesses.* Harvard House Publishers.
2. Carrie Underwood. Azlyrics.com,
   https://www.azlyrics.com/lyrics/carrieunderwood/jesustakethewheel.html.
3. D. L. Moody. Sermon Quotes, https://sermonquotes.com/trouble/14346-i-have-more-trouble-with-d-l-moody-than-with-any-other-man-ive-ever-met-dwight-l-moody.html.
4. Bill Bright. Cross Walk. The story of two dogs,
   https://www.crosswalk.com/devotionals/insights-from-bill-bright/the-story-of-two-dogs-dec-24.html.

Chapter 8. Reward of the GIFT

1. C.T. Studd. *Only one life*, https://tonycooke.org/stories-and-illustrations/only-one-life/.
2. Jim Hill. *What a day that will be*, https://namethathymn.com/christian-hymns/what-a-day-that-will-be-lyrics.html.
3. Steve and Annie Chapman. *Season of a man,*
   https://www.steveandanniechapman.com/2013/01/26/seasons-of-a-man/.

172

About the Author

Like you, John Bentley has experienced the ups and downs of life. One moment you are on cloud nine, at other times you become confused not quite sure of where to turn next. Through it all John has come to understand that allowing the Holy Spirit to lead you is the key to becoming a bold, effective Christian who rises above anger, fear, depression, and selfishness to further God's kingdom.

John's aha moment came early in his Air Force career when he received feedback that his leadership style under pressure was like someone opening a coke can after it was shaken. This led him on a journey to discover why he behaved poorly in tough situations. The findings John uncovered were not easy to accept, but he possessed the desire to learn and willingness to overcome limiting beliefs that caused him to continually struggle, be frustrated, and limit his opportunities for success.

After he retired from the Air Force, John founded Power 2 Transform. Since 2003 his sole focus is on teaching people how to master self-leadership especially when faced with adversity. His goal whether speaking, coaching or training is always the same –

equipping people to think clearly, behave wisely and model success so they can use their talents to serve others and glorify God.

John authored the book, *52 Ways to Motivate Yourself, The Power of Humility* and is featured in the book *Speaking of Success.* In this book, John shares the 5 Enablers of Success along with other business experts such as Ken Blanchard (The One-Minute Manager), Jack Canfield (Chicken Soup for the Soul), and Stephen Covey (The 7 Habits of Highly Successful People). John is also a contributor to audio program, *17 Biblical Principles of Success,* offering candid conversation with 50 other faith and life veterans with experience in business.

John is married to Laura Bentley. They have 4 adult children, Krista, Jennifer, Kelly and Mike along with three grandsons, Alex, Cohen and Kaiden. John and Laura reside in Hartselle, AL.

Invite John to Speak

You Are A GIFT
Key Verses: Genesis 1:27, 1 Peter 4:10

Do you often ask yourself, "What is my God-given purpose?" Through the death of his adult daughter John found the answer. This program is filled with thought provoking stories and practical steps to help you reflect God's Image and Fulfill your Talent in service to others allowing you to live your purpose and glorify God.

Rejoice in the Lord, Always
Key Verse: Philippians 4:4

Many of us become discouraged and don't know where to turn when faced with the problem's life puts in our path. This program teaches us how to lean on God and rejoice as the Holy Spirit transforms us more into the likeness of Christ with each difficulty that comes our way.

Transformed by the Spirit
Key Verse: 2 Corinthians 5:17

God wired you with distinct strengths, but also weaknesses that hold you prisoner to your flesh. This program will help you learn how God transformed Paul, Peter, Abraham and Moses' natural weaknesses. By submitting to the Holy Spirit, they became bold, effective Christians who rose above anger, fear, depression, and selfishness to further God's Kingdom.

175

John's Contact Information

Email: john@youareagift.foundation

Phone: 256-612-0015

www.youareagift.foundation

www.johnbentleyspeaks.com